Rhondda MacKay

P9-DJK-052

THE emerging CHURCH

Also by Bruce Sanguin:

Darwin, Divinity, and the Dance of the Cosmos: An Ecological Christianity

Summoning the Whirlwind: Unconventional Sermons for a Relevant Christian Faith

Also from the Experience! Faith Formation Curriculum for Adults series:

Experiencing an Ecological Christianity
based on *Darwin, Divinity, and the Dance of the Cosmos*

BRUCE SANGUIN

The
emerging
Church

A Model
for Change
&
a Map
for Renewal

CopperHouse

Editor: Michael Schwartzentruber
Cover and interior design: Verena Velten
Cover photo: © Creatas/maXx images
Prepress Production: Chaunda Daigneault
Proofreader: Dianne Greenslade

Unless otherwise noted, all scripture quotations are from the New Revised Standard Version of the Bible, copyright 1989 by the Division of Christian Education of the National Council of Churches of Christ in the USA. All rights reserved. Used by permission.

Quotations from the Revised Standard of the Bible, copyright 1946, 1952, 1971 by the Division of Christian Education of the National Council of Churches of Christ in the USA. All rights reserved. Used by permission.

CopperHouse is an imprint of Wood Lake Publishing, Inc. Wood Lake Publishing acknowledges the financial support of the Government of Canada, through the Book Publishing Industry Development Program (BPIDP) for its publishing activities. Wood Lake Publishing also acknowledges the financial support of the Province of British Columbia through the Book Publishing Tax Credit.

At Wood Lake Publishing, we practise what we publish, being guided by a concern for fairness, justice, and equal opportunity in all of our relationships with employees and customers. Wood Lake Publishing is an employee-owned company, committed to caring for the environment and all creation. Wood Lake Publishing recycles, reuses, and encourages readers to do the same. Resources are printed on 100% post-consumer recycled paper and more environmentally friendly groundwood papers (newsprint), whenever possible. A percentage of all profit is donated to charitable organizations.

Library and Archives Canada Cataloguing in Publication
Sanguin, Bruce, 1955-
The emerging church : a model for change & a map for renewal / Bruce Sanguin.
Includes bibliographical references.
ISBN 978-1-55145-566-2
1. Church renewal. 2. Religion and science. 3. Emerging church movement. I. Title.
BV600.3.S23 2008   262.001'7   C2008-900463-9

Copyright © 2008 Bruce Sanguin
All rights reserved. No part of this publication may be reproduced – except in the case of brief quotations embodied in critical articles and reviews – stored in an electronic retrieval system, or transmitted in any form or by any means, electronic, mechanical, photocopying, recording, or otherwise, without prior written permission of the publisher or copyright holder.

Published by CopperHouse
An imprint of Wood Lake Publishing Inc.
9590 Jim Bailey Road, Kelowna, BC, Canada, V4V 1R2
www.woodlakebooks.com
250.766.2778

Printing 10 9 8 7 6 5 4 3 2 1
Printed in Canada by Houghton Boston

To my mother, Betty, a resilient spiritual pilgrim
who has never quite given up on the church.

contents

Gratitudes

Sometimes, the heart of a book waits until you think you've finished writing to make an appearance. That's when the realization hits you that you've merely made a good start. Readers of the early manuscript are the first to deliver the message that you are not quite as done writing as you might have hoped. I want to thank all of you for the gracious and unique ways you each conveyed this news. Thank you for the gift of your time, careful reading, and comments: Heather Burton; Anna Christie; Ann Evans; Natalie Hall; Melinda Munro; Jeff Seaton; and Angela Verbrugge.

I want to especially thank George Eddey, my friend from Ohio, who was the first to read the early manuscript, and who has been a tireless supporter and promoter of my work. I also wish to thank my editor, Mike Schwartzentruber, who once again brought his wisdom, clarity of thought, and editorial acumen to the task with characteristic grace and skill.

I have been influenced by many wonderful souls, including Matthew Fox, who was the first to validate my intuition of the shortcomings of a redemption-centred paradigm, and to turn my heart and mind to the mystery of creation and creativity; Brian Swimme, who deconstructed the scientific materialism of my secular education, and the theistic theological models of my religious education, with a scientific/sacred cosmology that spoke to my soul; Marcus Borg, who has helped to provide countless congregations in North America with a new paradigm of Christian faith; and John Dominic Crossan, whose brilliance as a New Testament scholar brought Jesus alive for me. More recently, the integral philosophy of Ken Wilber has provided me with a map of reality that has opened up new worlds and new perspectives.

I would particularly like to thank Tom Bandy, who was the first to awaken me to the possibility of a different way of being the church. Early in my ministry he asked, "Why is the mainline church failing to thrive?" He stepped out from behind the safety of his national office desk and came, a prophet of hope, to congregations yearning for the abundant life of Christ. I want to thank Diana Butler Bass as well, whose careful research confirms that mainline Christianity is not quite ready to roll over and die, and that spiritual practice is at the heart of vital congregations.

My thinking has been shaped in the crucible of the three United Church of Canada congregations that I have served over the last 20 years: Centennial-Rouge; West Hill; and Canadian Memorial Church and Centre for Peace. I've been exceptionally lucky to serve these three communities of faith, each one willing to push at the edge of what it means to be "church." Each is filled with generous and loving souls who have made my ministry truly meaningful. The people of Canadian Memorial have been faithful and game partners for these last 12 years in experimenting with new ways of being the church. My heartfelt thanks to these congregations.

I end by thanking my wife, Ann Evans, for all her loving support. My books are written in the midst of leading a busy congregation. This means that my writing tends to leak over into our personal time, not only in terms of the hours spent on the computer and reading, but also in the inevitable intellectual preoccupation when I'm not engaged directly in these activities. Thank you, my love.

Prologue

ABUNDANT LIFE

I would rather be ashes than dust! I would rather that my
spark should burn out in a brilliant blaze than it should
be stifled by dry rot. I would rather be a superb meteor;
every atom of me in magnificent glow, than a sleepy and
permanent planet. Our proper functioning is to live, not to
exist. I shall not waste my days in trying to prolong them.
I shall use my time.

~ JACK LONDON ~

I want our churches to be fully alive. In John's gospel, Jesus is reported
to have said that he came to bring abundant life. You can measure the
health of a congregation using this criterion. Where are the signs of
life? Almost 25 years ago, an itinerate evangelist persuaded me that
Jesus was the way, the truth, and the life. So I took the plunge and asked
Christ to break open my timid heart. My life has never been the same.
I've since shed the beliefs associated with my evangelist friend, but not
the heart-breaking, hcart-healing love that turned my life upside down.

I wanted to give my life back to the one who had offered me my own, and so I decided to serve the church as an ordained minister.

I have now spent over 20 years in that role. What I look for in congregations are companions who wake me up, who challenge me by their very presence to put my nets out into deeper waters, and who have traded in respectability for a divine love. I want to be that kind of presence for others as well. Can we be the radiant presence of the Christ for each other and for the world? A poem by the 14th-century Sufi mystic, Hafiz, captures my yearning for the church.

A One-Story House

I am glad
* that my Master lived*
In a one-story
House

When I began to traverse
The early stages of
Love.

For when he would speak
Of the wonders and
* the beauty of creation,*

When he began to reveal
The magnificent realities
* of God*

I could not control
* my happiness*
And would commence
An ecstatic dance

That almost always
* resulted in a*
Tremendous encore –

A dive, head first,
Out of his
Window.

Hafiz,
The Friend was very kind
* to you*
During those early years

And you only broke your
* big nose*
Seventeen times![1]

We don't have to be diving out of our stained glass windows or doing back flips down the centre aisles to show that we're alive. There are quieter forms of witness that are lively expressions of the Spirit. But let's remember that, right from the start, the public accused our spiritual ancestors of drunken behaviour – at nine o'clock in the morning! The church was born in the ecstasy of abundant life. What a confession that we reserve one Sunday a year for Pentecost! Jesus' followers were ecstatic and they couldn't keep it in.

I want to help our congregations to be alive – to be centres of authenticity, vitality, and creativity. I want to be with others who drink deeply from the well of living waters and then make a Christ-shaped offering of all the nourishment they've received. In other words, I want to be with those who want to make a difference in the world. There is so much untapped potential in our congregations.

Jesus unfurled the scroll of Isaiah one day in the synagogue and read from a section in which Isaiah makes the bold claim that the Spirit of the Lord was upon him – to change the world: to make it so that the poor heard good news; to see to it that everybody had a piece of land to call their own so that they could feed their family; he imagined the lame doing a jig, and the blind opening their eyes to the magnificence of life. To cap it all off, Jesus said that this was happening *through* him (Luke 4:18–19)! And, if you intended to follow him, it would happen through you as well. In my books, that constitutes a life worth living and a vision for the church.

Many congregations are struggling to find the abundant life that Christ offers. Over the years, we have formed some bad habits that now get in the way of divine abundance. We have become overly bureaucratic – too many meetings and not enough ministry happening. We have substituted busyness for the real business of the church – helping people to come alive in Christ. Clergy have exhausted themselves being personal chaplains for far too many families, rather than being exemplars of abundant life. In the mainline church, we have lost the practice of prayer and have replaced it with programs that aren't

Exemplars of Abundant Life

necessarily related to a clear mission and vision. We have made being warm and friendly with newcomers our primary purpose, when in fact they are looking for the Holy Spirit. We have associated the Christian· life with "being good" forgetting that it is about being in God. We have developed cultures of superficiality. We have learned to be civil and courteous with the person sitting beside us in church, but we don't take the opportunity to hold them in their brokenness and dance with them in their joy. Somewhere along the line, we have forgotten our own sacred story found in scripture and so have become susceptible to the dominant cultural narratives competing for our allegiance.

The good news is that bad habits are possible to break! As liberator, Christ can set us free!

Jesus tells a parable about a dishonest steward who gets wind that he's about to be fired (Luke 16:1–13). Immediately the steward gets down to business – taking care of his own butt in preparation for the axe to fall. He is shrewd to the point of dishonesty. Shockingly, Jesus doesn't condemn the man's behaviour in the parable. This doesn't mean, however, that Jesus is recommending that "the children of light" replicate this man's methods. Rather, Jesus is challenging his followers to act as decisively and resolutely in the face of a crisis as this shady character did.

In my corner of the world, the public has metaphorically fired the mainline church. They've sent a message saying that they will no longer be needing our services, thank you very much – at least not as we've been delivering them. For many reasons, mainstream culture has decided that we've squandered the sacred treasure and are no longer fit to be stewards of the Holy One's affairs. Those interested in spirituality are fleeing to the mountains and forests, to Buddhist temples, or to the sanctuary of a yoga studio. These are, unquestionably, sacred venues where the all-pervasive Spirit moves. But we need to sort out – *now* – exactly what *our* business is, and then get to work with a holy shrewdness.

The steward in Jesus' parable had a window of opportunity. He took a realistic look at his capacities and realized that he was too old to dig ditches and too proud to beg for a living. He had to think on his feet and come up with a strategy. The master ultimately praised his ingenuity, even though it came at the master's own expense. Again, Jesus is not condoning the dishonest man's methods. He's challenging his followers to be as bold and ingenious as those whose motivations are not grounded in Spirit. There's still time for us to rediscover new life in Christ. As stewards of the Holy One's treasure, we need to make an honest assessment of where we're at, and then be bold about reclaiming the abundant life Christ offers.

Almost 20 years ago, I listened to theologian and priest Matthew Fox speak of the shift from a redemption-centred paradigm, focused on original sin, to a creation-centred paradigm, focused on original blessing. The former focused on what God accomplished on our behalf through Jesus Christ, while the latter focuses on what God *is accomplishing* through us – the new thing God is doing.

This struck a chord deep within me. Rooted in Christ, this model challenges us to ask: What is the future that needs us in order to emerge? Disciples in the emerging church are centres of Spirit-animated creativity. Furthermore, this model grounds us in our deep connection with the planet and with all creation.

Then, a decade ago, physicist Brian Swimme and cultural historian and Roman Catholic priest Thomas Berry helped me to view the evolutionary story of the universe as a sacred narrative that connects all creation, all people, and all cultures. The faith systems of the world, including the Christian tradition, are a part of this evolving story. In my book *Darwin, Divinity, and the Dance of the Cosmos: An Ecological Christianity*, I set the sacred story of our faith in dialogue with the sacred story of creation.

The church itself is part of this ongoing evolutionary story. We are meant to evolve, in a Christ-informed way, along with the rest of the universe, and according to the fundamental principles of nature. This evolutionary paradigm invites us to be in conversation with scientific culture and to look at the evolving life of our congregations through both a biblical and a scientific lens. In this book, I use scientific as well as theological language to describe the process by which congregations evolve. At the same time, I have tried to make this language accessible to people like myself, a non-scientist. One of the scientific principles that is central to this work is called *creative emergence*, which I describe in Chapter 1. An emerging congregation evolves within a creation-centred, evolutionary paradigm.

For some, this language may seem overly abstract. Yet my intent is not abstraction. On the contrary, I intend this book to work as a very practical model for congregational culture shifting. I offer a map of some of the principles and practices that have helped to open the gates of life and love in Christ, in the congregations I have served. Please remember, though, that the map itself is an evolving reality. Some of the practices I advocate are just that: practice! In an emergent paradigm, congregations enjoy the freedom to fail – to try new things out, to assess their viability, and then to try again. You are free to try these ideas, tweak them, or toss them. The fundamental characteristic of this Spirit-infused, evolutionary universe is creativity. This is what we need to light up our congregations – permission to be centres of creative discipleship.

I wrote this book for church leaders, both lay and clergy, who are ready to act as guides on this journey of congregational renewal. Sometimes I slip into addressing clergy more directly. When this happens, I hope that the lay reader will enjoy overhearing the conversation. Everything I share with clergy applies also to lay congregational leaders.

I should also say that I wrote from the context of having served primarily in urban settings, although my first congregation was a tiny church around which the city grew up. By the standards of most mainline congregations in my country, the congregation I currently serve is relatively affluent. Our challenges and opportunities therefore reflect this culture. If you are in a rural setting, or part of a congregation that is struggling simply to pay your minister's salary, translating some of my observations and strategies into your context may be challenging at times. Nevertheless, the spiritual principles upon which this model of congregational transformation is constructed are universal. While I don't address it in the book, this model requires neither paid clergy nor a building in which to worship. The abundant life of Christ breaks out whether two or three, or two or three hundred, or two or three thousand souls open their hearts.

I believe in the power of these Christ-centred souls to make a difference in a hurting world. If we are to survive as a species, God needs us to help the human race grow into the humility of the Christ. We're crowding out other life forms on the planet, and degrading our bio-systems as we multiply our species at unsustainable rates. We've just come out of the most violent century in the history of humanity, and we don't appear to be off to a better start in the 21st century. In the aftermath of 9-11, the lines have been drawn between "us" and "them." The Middle East is a tinderbox. The gap between the obscenely wealthy and the desperately poor is widening. Economic globalism, the imperialism of the 21st century, demands our allegiance, and assures us that perpetual economic growth defines the purpose of human existence and will save us if we just trust it. In the Western world, narratives of consumerism and the cult of celebrity are draining souls of all meaning and purpose. Now more than ever God is calling us to come alive to our deep purpose.

I pray that this book helps your congregation live up to its high and holy calling to be the living presence of the Christ in the world. If it helps to spark your holy shrewdness and radiant creativity, I will be gratified.

---

[1] Hafiz, *The Gift: Poems by Hafiz*, Daniel Ladinsky, trans. (New York: Penguin Press, 1999), 176.

one

Growing from the Inside Out: The Principle of Emergence

Like living stones, let yourselves be built into a spiritual house…
~ 1 PETER 2:5 ~

The kingdom of God is within you.
~ LUKE 17:21 ~

This is a dream that came to a member of our planning team just as we were launching a congregational renewal program. It's in two parts.

In the first scene, people are standing around a very large, grey stone admiring its size and physical beauty. They are going on and on about how great it looks. The dreamer is surprised by their fascination with its exterior characteristics. Yes, the rock is beautiful, she agrees. But the *real* beauty, she tries desperately to explain to the crowd, is radiating from *within* the rock. A radiant, palpable energy was apparent to her, but not to the gathering. The stone was *alive*, from the inside out.

Scene two repeats the theme. Another group is standing around a brand new, shiny car. They are running their hands along the sleek contours, admiring the leather seats and the elegant design features of the dashboard. Again, the dreamer approaches them, amazed by how their fixation on the exterior beauty has blinded them to the real attraction. She draws their attention to the set of keys in the ignition and tells them that they haven't seen anything yet. It's what's *under* the hood that counts. The car has actual *power*. "If this fancy exterior is lighting up your eyes," she says, "wait until you turn the key and discover the power *within!*"

Our planning team interpreted the dream as a sacred gift, meant to inform our congregational journey of culture shifting. The congregation I currently serve, Canadian Memorial United Church, worships in a turn-of-the-century, grey stone building famous for its stained glass windows, its three manual Casavant organ, and the beauty of the sanctuary. Clearly, the rock in the first scene of the dream represented the enchanting exterior physical characteristics of the church building. Over the years, the sanctuary has been a stop for tour groups visiting historical sites. The congregational members have been faithful and responsible stewards of the building. But the challenge for every generation is to pay at least as much attention to the stewardship of its *inner* life – the spirit within all of us, as we open ourselves to the transforming power and wisdom of the Christ. The challenge for our team would be to ignite the *inner* radiance of our life together as a congregation.

The early church was no different. It was forced to contend with the reality that Temple worship in Jerusalem could no longer be the defining characteristic of its spiritual life. Holy pilgrimages to this sacred site were a thing of the past. It wasn't only that the followers of Jesus were no longer welcome. After 70 CE, there *was* no Temple! The Romans had destroyed it. It would never be rebuilt.

Now that the dwelling place of God had been destroyed, where would they find their spiritual centre? They would find it *within*. They would become, in the words of the author of 1 Peter, the "living stones" of the new temple. As Jesus' followers accessed their inner power, the new movement would be built from the inside out. This was the "key" that galvanized this little band of nobodies and empowered them to spread throughout the Roman Empire. They discovered their own inner radiance, sustained and shaped by the power of the living Christ.

It's difficult to break out of the mentality that the "church" is the building. That favourite Sunday-school hymn, "I am the church, you are the church, we are the church together,"[1] got it right. But getting people to believe it is another thing. Begin a conversation about amalgamating with another congregation or moving the location of the church building, and this will become immediately evident. But even when we understand that the church is not the building, very quickly other inviolate structures will surface: our organizational model, the time of the worship service, the pews, the hymns, and, of course, that structural catch-all, "the way we've always done it." When the members of a congregation really get that they are *themselves* the radiant presence of the Christ, they begin to attend as carefully to their inner radiance as they do to the outer reality of their structures.

Our primary model for this inside-out dynamic of coming to life is the universe itself. It's been in the process of increasing its capacity for abundant life for 14 billion years: hydrogen and helium atoms organize themselves into stars; stars organize themselves into galaxies; and galaxies organize themselves into solar systems. And in one of those solar systems our planetary home came to life. When it did, there was no stopping the evolutionary march, from bacteria right through to the animal kingdom and the emergence of the human being. With the arrival of the human being, the universe gained the capacity to observe itself – a stunning achievement.

The universe did all of this without a blueprint, from the inside out. Scientists call this dynamic, by which the universe winds itself up in the direction of more abundant life, *creative emergence*. Hydrogen and oxygen find each other, and from their dance an entirely novel thing emerges that makes life possible: water. Nobody could have predicted water from the individual qualities of these two molecules. Creative emergence affirms that not only is the whole greater than the sum of its parts, it is completely, unpredictably, new and more complex. This new "whole" – water – would eventually take its place as a *part* of some new, unpredictable, and more complex whole. This is how the universe evolves.

This ongoing evolutionary dynamic of creative emergence is a fundamental dynamic of life itself and therefore applies every bit as much to congregational life as it does to nature. Congregations become potential centres of creative emergence when they consciously align themselves with the evolutionary universe. The form of life that emerges in the church will be Christ-shaped.

Creation has a staggering creative capacity for innovation, adaptation, novelty, experimentation, and resiliency. It's a profound mystery to scientists from whence this capacity originates, and it's not their job to interpret it so much as to describe it. Theologians are left the task of interpretation. I name the source of this dynamic capacity *Spirit* – the inner power and radiance at the heart of the universe, which has a non-coercive, evolutionary bias toward what Jesus called "abundant life."

THE EMERGING CHURCH – A DEFINITION

Before I define what I mean by an emerging congregation, let me say a word about the metaphors of emergence currently in circulation these days. New Testament scholar and author Marcus Borg contrasts the *emerging* paradigm/church with the *earlier* paradigm/church.[2] He intends to remain non-judgmental about the earlier paradigm, which he pretty much equates with biblical literalism and atonement theology. By his definition, an emerging church – in other words, a church that embodies his emerging paradigm – appreciates metaphor and takes the Bible seriously, but not literally. Essentially, this is a church that has transcended mythic Christianity, although he doesn't use those words. Author and theologian Brian McClaren represents the so-called *emergent* church movement in the U.S. In my limited reading of this movement, McLaren appeals to Christians who are grounded in the earlier paradigm, but who want to inform their theology with a postmodern sensibility that takes seriously the importance of perspective and context in the search for truth. My definition complements these two current ways of defining emergence by bringing a scientific understanding of emergence to bear on the conversation.

In this book, when I talk about the *emerging* church I am referring, in a general sense, to congregations that are meeting the challenges of the postmodern world with creativity and vitality. An emerging congregation, by my definition, is one that is always looking out at the horizon for the future that desires to be born *through them*. They are aware that the Spirit-driven universe is evolving in and through their common life together. These congregations view their own co-creative capacity as a sign that the Spirit is active in their midst. More specifically, I am referring to congregations who are making a shift from a redemption-centred theological model to a creation-centred, evolutionary Christian theology. These congregations are *domains of creative emergence*, which I define in more detail below.

Science has now determined that the universe evolves geologically, biologically, and culturally. The spiritual realm of the Christian church is also part of this evolutionary dynamic. We are *meant* to evolve. If the Spirit is involved in the evolutionary process – as I believe is the case – then we need to start thinking about our lives in Christ through an evolutionary lens. When Jesus says, "consider the lily, how it *grows*" and then goes on to make his point that its beauty is effortless – a gift of this Spirit-infused universe – he is asking his disciples to consciously align themselves with this mysterious power of life. We *grow*!

Evolution is a built-in, gracious dynamic of God's universe. Jesus' parables and teachings are filled with this mystery. For example, Jesus compares the kingdom of God to the growth of a seed.

The kingdom of God is as if someone would scatter seed on the ground, and would sleep and rise night and day, and the seed would sprout and grow, he does not know how. The earth produces of itself, first the stalk, then the head, then the full grain in the head. But when the grain is ripe, at once he goes in with his sickle, because the harvest has come (Mark 4:26–30).

Jesus had no way of understanding plant growth or evolution scientifically, but it's implicit in this teaching. Notice his developmental perspective: first the stalk, then the head, and then the grain. We now understand that all growth, from biological to cultural to spiritual, evolves developmentally, with more complex forms of life emerging out of the foundation established by simpler forms.

Paul uses the metaphor of growth in Christ in an explicitly developmental, if not evolutionary, way: "When I was a child, I spoke like a child, I thought like a child, I reasoned like a child; when I became an adult I put an end to childish ways" (1 Corinthians 13:11). Psychological and spirituality maturity is an evolutionary feature of the universe, at the level of human development. In the process of maturation, humans move through specific stages, each laying down the foundation for the next, from infancy to adulthood. The writer of Colossians, likely a disciple of Paul's, tells his community that to be in Christ is to "grow with the growth that is from God" (Colossians 2: 1–19). They needed to let their beliefs and practices evolve in Christ. In other words, the "growth that is from God" is evolutionary in nature.

EMERGENCE

As a scientific principle, creative emergence is defined by three core dynamics.

1. Novelty: the whole that comes together from the parts is absolutely unpredictable. The new whole will be greater than the sum of the parts in a specific way – it will be more complex than the parts themselves and of a completely new order.

2. Self-organization: life knows how to wind itself up in the direction of increasing complexity, consciousness, beauty, and compassion. There is intelligence built into the fabric of the universe that defies

scientific explanation. In my previous book, *Darwin, Divinity and the Dance of the Cosmos: An Ecological Christianity*, I name this intelligence Sophia, the feminine personification of divine wisdom found in scripture (Proverbs 8).

3. Transcendence and inclusion: an organism, a system, or an individual grows by transcending yet including its constituent parts.

What I am proposing in this book is that we apply these evolutionary principles to congregational renewal – that is, that we intentionally create a culture that honours novelty and self-organization, and that is continually in the process of transcending yet including its own structures and systems in faithfulness to the abundant life Christ offers.

1. Novelty

We don't typically associate the institutional church with novelty! Yet what is clear from an evolutionary perspective is that novelty is the secret of life. It turns out that the prophet Isaiah described the creative activity of the Holy One exactly right, when on behalf of God he announces, "Behold, I am doing a new thing!... Do you not perceive it?" (Isaiah 43:19, RSV). For those with eyes to see, and hearts that are open, God is continually doing a new thing – through our congregations!

In other words, the universe is making it up as it goes along. Using theological language, the Spirit is genuinely surprised by the novelty and creativity that is emerging in each new life form. Every living system struggles and plays its way into an indeterminate future. We need, therefore, to give ourselves more permission to mimic this life process in our congregations.

Anthropologists have noticed that the period of play in mammals – in the first year of life typically – is the time when the species may actually stumble onto new adaptive behaviours that may be passed on to future generations. One of the unique qualities of human beings is that we have the capacity to extend this period of play over the course of our entire lives. Think about the need to adapt to the challenges of the 21st century as an opportunity to play with new forms. We may stumble onto new forms in the church by playing with the ever-renewing Spirit.

There are many church programs out there that promote what they claim is an ideal and universally applicable approach to church renewal. We're told we *must* organize around small groups, develop a worship band and use multimedia projection, or do an audit to determine if we have the five or ten marks of a healthy congregation. I've read many of these programs and have tried more than a few. Some have been helpful and I'll be recommending a few myself. But, in the end, *understanding and enacting the principle of emergence* is the key. This is the new wine that God is pouring out. Diversity appears to be a core expression of Spirit in our universe. Just look around! No two fingerprints are the same. Why would a congregation want to replicate another by adopting some "ideal" form or program? The forms known as "church" in the 21st century will be unique, surprising, and unpredictable.

The principal work of congregational transformation is to create a culture of dynamic emergence. St. Paul noticed that the Spirit worked to give faith communities exactly what they needed in order to thrive – Spirit-given gifts unique to each member. Together, these members constituted the living body of Christ.

We've tried to take this seriously at Canadian Memorial by developing an intentional process of discerning and deploying our gifts in the congregation and beyond. To give one example, after hearing me preach a sermon on the mystical tradition of our faith, a woman approached me. Her face was radiant. She knew how she wanted to use her gifts to build up the Body of Christ. In her professional life, she helped dog-owners communicate more effectively with their companion animals. Her idea was to combine her intuitive communication skills with animals and the mystical tradition within Christianity by offering groups for Christian pet owners. Now, I wouldn't have come up with this idea in a month of Sundays. Yet emergent cultures honour this kind of holy eccentricity and recognize it as the "new thing" God is doing.

At Canadian Memorial, we'll find a way to adapt to this woman's gifts and to support her passions. When we require our members to fit into pre-determined bureaucratic slots, we lose our eccentricity, the wild and unpredictable stirrings of Spirit.

2. Self-Organization

The Nobel laureate chemist Ilya Prigogine noticed that a system under pressure will reorganize itself at a higher, more complex level. It will "escape to a higher order" in order to deal with increased stress, stimulation, and information. Prigogine came up with the term *self-organization* to describe this capacity of an organism, system, or individual to reorganize itself in response to changing life conditions. Francesco Varela, a cognitive scientist, coined the term *autopoiesis* to describe essentially the same thing – the ability of life at all levels to self-renew or to make the changes necessary to become a fuller manifestation of itself.

Both of these terms are linguistic stabs at describing a profound mystery: life is continually in the process of organizing itself in the direction of increasing complexity, consciousness, beauty, and compassion. What leaves scientists baffled is that there is no external force driving this process. It is a built-in feature of the universe, a part of the fabric of the cosmos. Molecules, galaxies, cells, organisms, and social systems are graced by an intrinsic, intuitive intelligence that serves the evolutionary initiative or drive of the universe to become evermore elegant. There *is* another realm out there, but it is found *within* this one. Perhaps Jesus intuited this when he taught that the kingdom of God is *within* (Luke 17:21). We can trust that life knows how to do life – after all, it has been organizing itself for 14 billion years.

Religious institutions, including the church, sometimes act as though they exist to perpetuate a particular form across generations and centuries. This is, cosmologically speaking, weird behaviour. An emergent congregation reinvents itself from the inside out. The ancient Greeks called this inner life force *eros*. This is the impulse of all life forms to reach higher towards transcendence. The Greeks also had a word for a universal power that non-coercively reaches "down" in order to help all creation ascend to the next level towards transcendence: *agape*, or unconditional love. This upward reaching impulse (eros) and the Holy One's non-coercive downward reaching love (agape) are an eternal, ever-present, and sacred feature of our evolutionary universe. The one we call God manifests in the realm of time and space *in* and *through* the evolution of life in all realms. This irrepressible impulse is holy, the presence of Wisdom, and is fully embodied in human form in Jesus of Nazareth.

The central thesis of this book is that the church of the 21st century must tap into this ancient, ever-renewing wisdom, if we are to thrive and not just survive. Conscious evolution – trusting and cooperating with this universal sacred wisdom – is the way forward.

The church of the 21st century is undergoing significant stress. The dynamic of self-organization tells us that if we can resist the temptation to retreat into survival mode, this stress contains the energy required to help us reorganize at a more complex level. It can actually be the signal that we need to allow new systems, new ways of governing, new educational programs, and new leadership models to emerge. The challenge is to develop congregational cultures and structures that are congruent with this emergent dynamic. This will entail shifting from cultures of command and control to cultures of self-organization. We need to be able to trust that new forms will emerge to help us "escape to a higher order." These new forms will allow the wine of the evolutionary Wisdom, known in Christ, to flow freely.

Recently at Canadian Memorial, our office administrator announced that she was leaving for another job – in two weeks! She was the hub of our congregation, a one-person information highway. Her announcement threw us into chaos. But an interesting thing began to *emerge*. Our part-time staff of four or five people, who were familiar with our operations, took over. I watched from the sidelines as they called impromptu meetings to determine who was doing what and what was falling through the cracks. They left each other messages at the end of their shift about what needed to be done. Most importantly, they began to develop new systems for dealing with the frenzy of the office. My personnel team would check in with me to see how things were going. Things were going great – and nobody was in charge! It was a beautiful thing to watch this group of people *self-organize* under the pressure of a crisis. We'll see in a later chapter that there are certain boundaries that need to be put in place, but once this is done we can observe and learn this life lesson of the universe – that cultures of command and control actually get in the way of the new thing that wants to emerge.

3. Transcendence and Inclusion

The universe responds to adaptive challenges or changing life conditions by evolving in a way that transcends yet includes previous forms. Through a process Ken Wilber calls "development through envelopment," all of life incorporates the adaptive intelligence of earlier life forms by enveloping them within a new and more complex form. This is the genius of DNA, whereby genes store memories of what has worked in the past and pass them on to subsequent generations. Yes, new forms emerge. But the point is this: everything that has worked in the past is brought forward into the future. This is the good news for those who are frightened by change because they worry about what might be lost. Nothing – at least nothing that worked – is ever lost. It's carried forward, transcended *and* included in the new form. On the other hand, in an evolutionary universe, *form fetish kills!*

This is true at all levels. Originally, a single cell without a nucleus (prokaryote) ran the show. But then it synergistically teamed up with other bacteria and became a multi-celled, nucleated bacteria (eukaryote). In other words, it developed by being enveloped. In our own bodies, vestiges of a particular form of bacteria with a whip-like tail are carried forward and take their place in the tail of a sperm cell, in our nerve-endings, and in the lining of our esophagus. Truly useful forms are never left behind. They are taken up as parts in a larger whole. The trick is in discerning what is "truly useful."

When Canadian Memorial was built in 1925, the founder decided that he would build the community centre first and *then*, five years later, the sanctuary. This was a powerful witness that the central value of this congregation would be "community first." That community centre literally became the centre of community life. It had one of the first indoor swimming pools in Vancouver. People still talk about their whole family taking swimming lessons at that pool.

Eleven years ago, facing seismic upgrading costs of over three million dollars, the congregation made the difficult decision to sell the historic building and, with the proceeds, to build a new but smaller centre on property adjacent to it. Letting go of that historic building, with all its memories, was painful for most people in the congregation. But the spirit of that building was not lost; the ethos implicit in the decision to serve the community by building it first was carried over into the new structure. The congregation decided to name it The Centre for Peace, making an explicit connection with the founding vision of the congregation – to work for peace in memory of those who lost their lives in W W I.

Structure and form are nothing more than physical manifestations of an intention or a function, in this case to serve the community. The new building was a new and more focused expression of the historic value to put community first. Today, The Centre for Peace hosts yoga, Tai Chi, Buddhist and Christian meditation, Reiki and Healing Touch, holistic tutoring, chanting festivals from all traditions, seminars on personal growth, and conferences on peace – to name just a few groups. The public now refers to Canadian Memorial as the "peace church."

The Centre for Peace transcended, yet included, the original intention of its founder to serve the community. The congregation decided to make a rather large change, but not for the sake of change itself. Rather, *it changed in order to become more of itself – autopoiesis* in action! – a fuller manifestation of what God was calling this community of faith toward.

This is the principle of evolutionary emergence at work: new forms emerge that build upon previous forms, taking them in the direction of increased capacity for the abundant life Christ offers.

This is also the context for the endless and often tedious conversations about tradition versus traditionalism. The unfolding universe is our model for community life. For 14 billion years, the universe has been evolving in and through a delicate balance of tradition and innovation. Tradition is valued in a cosmological context by carrying forward what worked – on the biological level in our DNA; and on the social-cultural level, through social conditioning, education, and the passing on of value systems. What *is* tradition if not the result of previous innovations that served the evolutionary purposes of life? What *is* innovation if not the evolution of tradition? Today's innovations will become tomorrow's traditions. Tradition*ism,* on the other hand – clinging to past forms – is a death sentence in an evolutionary model.

To become attached to a particular form in an evolutionary context is to die out. The same dynamic applies to congregational life. The one big difference is that because we have the gift of conscious self-awareness, we can *consciously* participate in the evolutionary thrust of the universe (the life of the Spirit). We can learn to be master-adapters. Just as corporations have learned to adapt with such innovations as "just-in-time" production (rather than filling up warehouses with product), so the church needs to tap into our highly evolved capacity to adapt and innovate. The emerging congregation intentionally fosters this culture of innovation.

The church of the 21st century will come back to life by mimicking the Spirit-infused dynamics of the evolutionary universe. We will embrace novelty, the wild and unpredictable stirrings of the Spirit. We will trust, as much as possible, the dynamic of self-organization, shifting from cultures of command and control to cultures of emergence. Finally, we will relax into the inevitability of evolutionary change in our congregations by trusting that no effective structure and useful tradition will ever be jettisoned. They may be transcended, but at the same time, they will be brought forward to serve the intentions of the living Christ.

FROM REDEMPTION TO CREATION

Historically, the church has operated out of a theological model focused more on our need for redemption than on our creative capacity. In the redemptive model, God acts primarily to save humans from sin. Our primary role is to receive this gracious gift and to act accordingly.

In this model, Jesus' role was to "come to earth" to rescue us from the clutches of Satan and from death itself. The church's focus, therefore, has been on an event 2000 years ago that saved us: Jesus' death on the cross. Even liberal churches tend to look backward at what God "did" for us in Jesus. When we talk about *revelation* – the theological doctrine of how we know God – we once again have a tendency to look to the past, to what God "has done" in Christ.

Because of this, church services sink inevitably into a passive stance, reciting what God has done *for* us and expressing gratitude for *God's* actions – actions unilaterally taken on our behalf. *Our* actions, we've been told, are what got us in trouble in the first place. The best we can do, therefore, is to fall in line and exercise obedience to God's will. We are *recipients,* not actors, in the redemptive model. Passive belief – that Jesus died for our sins – along with obedience, will get us a ticket to heaven.

This paradigm is not so much about our growth in Christ as it is about believing in this model or doctrine of redemption. All the important stuff was accomplished 2000 years ago, and we're just waiting for God to come and finish the job. This model can subtly insinuate itself into our mission, vision, values, and governance.

Admittedly, this is an oversimplification. But it's not far off the mark. There's something missing in this theological model – two things actually.

The first thing that's missing is a sense of natural grace, an understanding that God works through natural processes, the *ever-*

present evolutionary dynamics of a gracious universe. Paul confesses as much in his sermon to the Athenians: "In God we live and move and have our being" (Acts 17:28). If God is known in creation through natural grace, then revelation is an ongoing process; as the universe evolves we come to know God more perfectly, as St. Paul affirmed (1 Corinthians 13:12). I've already referred to the metaphor of growth in Jesus' teachings: seeds that grow mysteriously on their own, the importance of the fertility of soil for the growth of the seed, the futility of a fig tree that doesn't grow, mustard plants that spread wildly, rising bread, and the beauty of a lily, to name a few. Can we trust that this non-coercive evolutionary bias for increased complexity, consciousness, and compassion is at work in creation *and* in congregations – today?! Can we reclaim Paul's insight that the Christ who is cosmic in scope is the organizing principle of this process (Colossians 1:15–20)?

The second missing element, flowing from the first, is that the redemptive model ignores our own creativity as a reflection of divine grace. The creative unfolding of the universe happens through *each of us*. To align oneself with this creative power is to be "turned on" and lit up from within. To appreciate that the future is emerging through *us* is to be "rich toward God" (Luke 12:21).

Don't get me wrong. It's important to look back, to remember Jesus' life, death, and resurrection. But *we look back as a way of looking forward*. Nobody, says Jesus, who puts his hand to the plough and looks back is fit for the kingdom of God (Luke 9:62). The fundamental orientation of Christian spirituality is forward-looking. We presence, as in pre-sense, and then enact the new thing God is doing in the world. Followers of Christ are those who lay down the furrows in which the seeds of the future are planted and take root. In this orientation, Jesus, as historical figure, acts as an icon. By gazing intently upon his life and teachings, the Holy Presence shines through and animates us, here and now, to make of our own creativity an offering to the world. The Christ is uniquely present in Jesus of Nazareth *and* cosmic in scope, encompassing the entire 13.7 billion years of evolution, and counting.

Thus, the Christ "event" is an ongoing emerging process that animates disciples in every age.

In a theological model that focuses on our creative capacity as a gift of God, we don't ignore the shadow side of humanity. We recognize that we are always falling short of God's intentions for us, not to mention falling short of our own potential (being made in God's image). But our problem is not innate sinfulness. It's foolishness. We've lost our way, as Jesus the wisdom teacher repeatedly taught. What we need is spiritual wisdom, not the removal of original sin. This spiritual wisdom comes from our scriptural tradition, from the wisdom traditions of other faith systems, from creation, and from the scientific understanding of the evolving universe.

Spiritual wisdom

As for sin – actions that flow from being out of right relationship with God, self, neighbour, and the earth, and that consequently curtail the Holy One's creative intentions – Jesus had a sure fire way of dealing with it. He forgave sin. No muss. No fuss. No animal slaughter. No priests need apply. Before one drop of his blood was ever shed on the cross, he liberated those who were oppressed by the label of "sinner," by forgiving them (Luke 7:48). And then he told his followers to do the same – seven times 70 times – whatever it takes to return human beings to their creative potential and inner radiance, by which the Holy One is glorified. We are redeemed through forgiveness not because redemption is an end in itself, but so that we may be liberated to become centres of creative emergence. Forgiveness is an act of creation in this model.

Congregations that are domains of creative emergence celebrate creativity as a sign of the Spirit's presence. Pentecost has been associated with fire for good reason. There has always been a primordial connection between fire and creativity. Everything we see around us, every thought we've ever had, every congregation that's ever worshipped, and every impulse to make the world a better place, came from fire – the originating fire of creation 14 billion years ago. What if we were to focus on the creative, Christ-shaped imaginations of those who follow Christ? What if we truly began to believe that the future will be determined by those with the most fertile imaginations and by those who deeply understand that we exist literally to co-create the future? Right now, our most creative minds are not necessarily focused on what is best for the earth and best for human dignity. Creativity that is harnessed for holy purposes, on other hand, can be a healing force. It is the radiance that lights us up from within, the key that unlocks our potential.

A STORY OF CREATIVE EMERGENCE

A woman calls and asks to have lunch with me. Martha is a new member of our congregation. She heard me speak in a sermon on a principle I learned from Bill Easum and Tom Bandy called "Ministry Anywhere, Anytime, by Anybody." We're sitting at the Picasso Café, a restaurant that trains at-risk youth. Before our salads arrive, Martha is telling me her story. She's a corporate lawyer and a Christian. She has just returned from the World Council of Churches in Africa. Her heart is broken open by the poverty she witnessed. She has a dream of creating a micro-banking project in one of the Townships outside of East London, South Africa. She has decided to leave her law practice to do this. I ask her what she needs. Martha tells me she needs $15,000 of seed money, and a team. Before we've finished our main course, I've committed myself to finding both the money and a team of people.

After eight years, The Townships Project continues to thrive (www.thetownshipsproject.org). African women are making their way out of poverty. Teams from Canadian Memorial make visits to the Township.

New life in Christ happens naturally, when you get out of the way. New ministries emerge and self-organize, through a dynamic of transcending yet including the traditions of the past.

The task of the church in the 21st century is a creative one – we must play our role in the reinvention of the human being. Father Thomas Berry describes the new age we are entering as Pax Gaia – the peace of the earth. This means not only peace between humans. It also means declaring a truce in the war we have been waging with the planet and with other-than-human creatures. As we enter this new era, Spirit is involved in equipping human beings for this mission.

It is time to proclaim with as much passion and elegance as we can muster that in Jesus, God *was* doing a new thing – and that through the living body of Christ, the church, God *is* doing a new thing. God is transforming lives in our congregations to take up this great mission, one disciple of Christ at a time, from the inside out. We can show how Christ, known in Jesus of Nazareth and in all of creation, is a unique and unrepeatable manifestation of the evolutionary Spirit. His passion for justice, his compassion for those left-behind, his capacity for authentic and abundant life, his mystical unity with God, his universal wisdom, and his willingness to give his life that we might find life – these are the holy qualities and characteristics of the life we are called to as his followers.

MAPPING IT OUT

1. *Self-organization:* Discuss a time in your life or in your congregation when it "all worked out." Can you identify a time when an increase in the level of stress helped you to "escape into a higher order," that is, to self-organize at an increased level of complexity?

2. *Transcend and include:* How is this conversation about tradition versus traditionalism going in your congregation? Think about your worship services, committee structures, and programs. Are there forms/structures that need to be left behind so that you can evolve? What needs to be transcended, yet included?

3. *Novelty:* What is the new thing that God is doing in your congregation? How did it come about? Do you feel free to play with new forms and structures?

---

[1] "We Are the Church," words and music by Richard Avery & Donald Marsh, 1972.
[2] Marcus Borg, The Heart of Christianity (New York: HarperCollins Publishing, 2003), xi–xv.

two

Shift Happens:
From Form-Fetish to
Function-First

[Mary] said to the stewards: "Do whatever he tells you."
~ John 2:5 (RSV) ~

"Rabbi, it is good for us to be here; let us make three dwellings,
one for you, one for Moses, and one for Elijah."
He did not know what to say, for they were terrified.
~ Mark 9:5–6 ~

The writer of John's gospel tells a story about Jesus turning water into fine wine at a wedding feast (John 2:1–11). Jesus' mother, Mary, notices that the wine has run out and turns to her son to do something about it. This is the event, according to John, that launches Jesus' ministry, the first of the signs that he is the Light and Love of God.

We're living in an age when the mainline church knows what it feels like to be the hosts of a wedding banquet when the wine runs out. Who hasn't felt a twinge of shame or embarrassment upon inviting a friend to a service of worship that ends up feeling more like a funeral than a celebration of Spirit? Or have we stopped inviting our friends to worship altogether? The first miracle Jesus performs is to keep a party going by helping the wine – the Spirit – to flow once again.

Jesus instructs the stewards to take the enormous jars, used traditionally for the rites of purification, and fill them with water. Witnesses must have thought that he intended to perform a traditional ritual. What else would one do with these jars except what you've always done with them? But in Jesus' revolutionary presence the jars have no intrinsic iconic status; they are functional, needed to serve a higher end, purveyors of "abundant life." (Imagine. Five hundred litres of wine!) Think about this next time the discussion comes around to removing the pews in your church and replacing them with comfortable chairs. Would Jesus look out upon our sanctuary and say, "Oh no, we're skuppered! Those pews have *always* been there." Or would he perform a "miracle," transforming the butt-buster pews into comfortable seats that could be removed to make space for youth to dance at a sacred rave? (A true miracle in many mainline churches!)

Imagine Jesus as church consultant. We've called him in because the wine has metaphorically run out: attendance is low, we're in the red financially, it's a sea of grey hair out there. So we take him on a tour of the church facilities. As we go, we tell him all about the congregation. He listens carefully as we explain our committee structure and the programs we're offering. It's risky business. The first thing he might do is look at us incredulously and ask, "You mean to say that you make everyone come to *you*? My friends and I were on the road constantly proclaiming the kingdom of God. Do you have a team of people making the good news known in the world?" Then it might get *really* uncomfortable. He might start asking about our committees. What exactly do they do? What difference are they making? On it goes, day after day, until he's satisfied he's got the picture. Now comes the consultant's report.

I'll leave it to your imagination what the report might contain. But rest assured Jesus will look upon our sacred cows like he looked upon those sacred purification jars. The only questions on his mind will be, "Does this serve abundant life? Do your structures, programs, and worship services help to keep the party going?"

John's story doesn't give us any details about those who may have been offended by using the jars of purification as containers for new wine. But you can bet there was grumbling. The congregation I serve did indeed have a conversation about removing the pews. One elderly woman got wind of it. She demanded a visit. I sat across from her in her living room, her body quivering in controlled rage as she solemnly swore that she would chain herself to a pew if we were to go forward. The pews are still there!

HAND-PICKING A THINK TANK

Nine months into my tenure, at a board retreat, I asked for permission to *handpick*, with the chair, a team of people we called the Think Tank. (Another congregation I know about called a similar team Vision Casters. Dream Team would be another good name.) I realize that this was an unusual request, and not one I would make in every situation. But too often, when we ask for volunteers, the same cast of characters ends up dominating the agenda – the very ones who have advanced symptoms of form fetish. An egalitarian ideal in the church can sometimes translate into the belief that everybody needs to be in on every single decision, and that anybody is able to volunteer for everything. The result is that nothing gets done, because it's too difficult to make decisions and the wrong people are in the right places. This is not democracy. It is group tyranny. In a true democracy, you trust your leaders, and if they betray that trust there are mechanisms for removing them from leadership. Think about authentic democracy as being about developing models of governance and ways of being together that ensure every single person will have equal opportunity to have their creativity nurtured and validated. I'm not recommending handpicking a Think Tank team in every situation. But sometimes, as Jesus taught, shrewdness is required, and there is biblical precedent.

Notice that when Jesus calls the 12 disciples he doesn't go into the local village and ask for a show of hands. He doesn't issue a general invitation asking who would like to join him. He *chooses* his disciples. He sees Nathaniel under a tree and senses that he is an honest man. He sees through Peter's bluster and into his rock-solid character, and discerns his capacity to withstand the coming storms. He sees that Mary and Martha, and many other women, have the qualities he's looking for in this new Spirit movement. He then invites these people to be his disciples. In the beginning, Jesus focused on getting the right people in the right places.

On another occasion, Jesus displays this same process of selecting certain individuals, when he chooses three of the 12 to accompany him up a mountain. He takes Peter, James, and John to give them a view from above. On the mountain, they see the transfigured Jesus having a chat with Moses and Elijah (Matthew 17:1–8). Still, they don't get it. This is a common theme in the gospels, precisely because it's so easy to get locked into old ways of doing things. The three disciples instinctually build three booths, one for each of the prophets. What they don't get is that Jesus isn't merely taking his place in a long line of prophets. As important as the work of Moses and Elijah was, Jesus is doing something new. He's building upon the work of his predecessors, yes – but duplicating it, absolutely not. Jesus is doing a new thing for a new age. Jesus wants them to see with new eyes. Building a different booth for each prophet, symbolizing evolutionary development, would have been a sign that they "got it." Even though they could not possibly have had an evolutionary perspective at this point in history, nevertheless Jesus' own consciousness is implicitly evolutionary. He wants them to see the new thing God is doing in and through his ministry. He is transcending yet including the prophetic work of Moses and Elijah. Think of this core team of leaders as the ones who will collectively take a high-level view of the life of your congregation.

When I arrived at Canadian Memorial, I was told that they had been through a visioning process. They had binders filled with the results of this process. I read through the notes, which contained information about new committees and who was going to serve on them, along with information about potential programs for the future. I appreciated for the spirit they conveyed. But one thing concerned me from the outset. The entire visioning process took place on a Saturday. In my 12 years with this congregation, I have met many truly remarkable, gifted people, and many committed souls. But nobody is gifted enough to complete a visioning process in a single day! I couldn't reconcile the process I had in mind when I was called to this community, and the one I was reading about in the binders. *Culture shift doesn't happen in a day. It doesn't happen in a year. Think ten years!*

Our new Think Tank team uncovered widespread confusion about the congregation's organizational model. Our most brilliant intervention was to do absolutely nothing. When the philosopher Nietzsche wrote that "chaos trusted becomes a dancing star," he was articulating one of the dynamics of emergence. Chaos theory describes "strange attractors." (There's the scientific attempt to describe Mystery again.) These attractors define a "basin of attraction," an inherent container within which a system in chaos may experiment with new forms of itself without totally dissipating. Chaos may be measured using mathematical models. Using supercomputers, it's possible to plot chaos. The really interesting thing is that when these strange attractors appear on a computer screen, they form exquisite patterns. Deep within the heart of reality – even in chaotic systems – lies what physicist David Bohn called an "implicate order." Is this what St. Paul meant when he named Christ as "the one in whom all things hold together" (Colossians 1:17)?

Chaos theory can help us not to panic. Working from an emergent paradigm, we chose to trust the chaos, the implicate order within the chaos of the system. For nine months we introduced no changes.

Congregational chaos is not the end of the world. Resist quick fixes. You'll make things worse. Step back. Trust that Christ is in the chaos, the hidden and invisible power of God making all things new. He is the beautiful pattern present, even when we see only chaos. Take time to cultivate relationships, discover the norms of the congregation, and keep an eye out for the natural leaders.

At the suggestion of Bill Easum, our Think Tank entered into a covenant, a sacred promise.[1] We agreed that nothing was sacred except for the gospel. Everything else was merely a vessel: the organ, the pews, the current organizational model, the role of clergy and lay people, the way we worshipped together, even our location! After all, what if amalgamating with another congregation served better the purposes of the gospel? What if we needed more parking? What if we didn't need a building to be the church? We agreed to assume the role of the steward in John's account of the wedding feast listening to whatever the living Christ told us to do – whatever it took to turn water into wine. Most importantly, we were serious.

In other words, form would reflect function. This can be frightening if generations of people have learned to confuse forms with the gospel of Christ. Remember the dream from Chapter 1? People were fixated on the beauty of the exterior of the car (the form), and in the process lost sight of the keys (access to the inner power). We do this all the time. For example, if you associate singing in worship with standing still and staring into a hymnbook, then clapping along to a hymn or allowing your body to move rhythmically to the beat may be threatening.

Introducing a natural metaphor may help people deal with their fear of change. Try setting the fear within a larger context. Have a conversation about how we all attained our current physical form: two legs, two arms, a torso, and a head with a three-tier brain. I have a calendar that features a different frog for each month of the year. The moment I saw February's frog (Dendrobates Tinctorius), all black with white spots, I thought "dairy cow." Darwin's insight that all biological life, including human life, derives from common stock means that all new forms invariably emerge out of previous forms. Emergent forms are organically connected to and grow out of previously existing forms. Nothing worthwhile is left behind in nature. *Nothing worthwhile will be left behind in the process of congregational culture shifting.*

All of us are concentrated amalgams of all the evolutionary forms that preceded us. We are all composed of the same elements forged in a supernova. Descendants of bacteria that lived four billion years ago are alive and well within our bodies – three pounds worth! We have 50–100 trillion cells that figured out how to cluster together to do a particular job on behalf of our bodies: digest, breathe, fight off disease, make proteins, eliminate, etc. On a physical level, we are who we are because the parade of life that preceded us has been open to 14 billion years of shape shifting in the service of life. We are built for change!

PARTS AND WHOLES

Jesus is our model. A few of the religious elite were threatened by his teaching. They felt that he was trying to replace their religion with some new-and-improved product. But Jesus told them that he had no desire to abolish the Law and the Prophets. Rather, he was trying to "fulfill" them – that is, express their interior dimension, the inner radiance that the Law and the Prophets point toward (Matthew 5:17). The powers correctly perceived that if they adopted his new teachings then what they considered to be the whole of the Law would become just one part of a larger whole. Jesus desired to connect the establishment with the inner life of the Law. In other words, he saw the radiance that others were missing.

Philosopher Ken Wilber says that reality itself consists of "whole/parts."[2] Every thing is at once a whole and at the same time a part of some larger whole. As a whole, the thing exhibits agency; it has a function and accomplishes this function. As a part, it exhibits communion; it functions as a part of a larger whole. Evolutionary theory states that wholes eventually end up being *parts* of yet larger wholes. Atoms are incorporated into molecules, molecules into cells, cells into organisms, and on and on. At all levels of creation – mineral, vegetable, plant, animal, human, social and cultural – when a whole actively either cannot or refuses to become a part of a larger whole, evolution grinds to a halt. Cancer is an example of a whole that refuse to function within the communion, that is, as a part of a larger whole. At the level of congregational life, the challenge is to help the current form of the congregation accept – and celebrate! – that it is always going to be a part of a larger emerging whole. Wholes eventually become parts of even larger wholes. Don't fight it.

The Think Tank may threaten some people because they are the first ones to recognize that the existing congregation – a whole in itself – exists to become a *part* of a larger whole. This larger whole is what the congregation will look like in the future. There will be those who are so comfortable with the status quo that they have no desire to become a mere part of something more comprehensive and new. But, in an evolutionary paradigm, this is just the way life develops. On behalf of the congregation, this team consciously pushes the boundaries of congregational self-definition. It regards previously sacred structures as interesting but limited expressions suited to earlier conditions. In so doing, the team is following the evolutionary bias of the Holy Spirit to co-create a new future.

A good leader serves two congregations: the one sitting in front of her on Sunday morning; and the one that is not yet present, the larger whole that will confer upon this current congregation "partial" status. This explains why cultivating a mission consciousness is so difficult in congregations. In our fear, we desire to freeze the existing configuration and call it complete. We want to be the whole, not a part of a larger whole. This is called idolatry and it's alive and well in our congregations. But the moment this kind of thinking creeps in, growth stops – both spiritual growth and the number of bums in the seats.

Jesus and all the angels are constantly telling his disciples to "fear not." Spirit is with us. Shift happens. But within all the changing forms, there are non-negotiable elements, as we will explore in the next chapter.

MAPPING IT OUT

1. Name the "sacred jars" that exist in your congregation, which the Christ may need to transform from iconic status to functional status so that you can serve the purpose of abundant life.

2. Imagine forming the equivalent of a Think Tank. What process will you use to choose this team? Why? Enter into a covenant, a sacred agreement, that you are willing to do whatever it takes to allow the emergent, abundant life of Christ to manifest.

3. Identify the chaos in your congregation. Can you imagine that Christ, as "strange attractor," can be located in the heart of this chaos? What would it mean to trust the chaos?

---

[1] Bill Easum, *Sacred Cows Make Gourmet Burgers* (Nashville: Abingdon Press, 1997), 131.
[2] Ken Wilber, *Sex, Ecology and Spirit: The Spirit of Evolution* (Boston: Shambhala, 1995), 45ff.

three

The Heart and Mind of Christ: Discerning Your Non-Negotiables[1]

Let the dead bury their own dead; but as for you, go and proclaim the kingdom of God.

~ LUKE 9:60 ~

First, Jesus handpicks 12 trusted disciples, his future leaders. Then, he spends time teaching them. They travel together, eat together, and live together in an intensive educational phase of coming to terms with Jesus' mission. This mission is summarized in a single metaphor – the kingdom of God. Jesus was not concerned with the form any future church might take. In fact, there's little evidence that he was much concerned with "church" at all. (Because of Jesus' relatively short ministry, he didn't have to deal with institutional matters, which fell to Paul.) But this much seems clear. The scaffolding of any future institution, had Jesus lived long enough to build one, would have been built upon the kingdom.

A word about the metaphor of the kingdom of God is necessary. There is no question that this is a patriarchal metaphor. It emerged in the context of a patriarchal culture after all: the Roman Empire. In *Darwin, Divinity, and the Dance of the Cosmos*, I suggest that we drop the "g" and change it to kin-dom of God. But let's first appreciate the edginess of the metaphor. Its power lies in the way it subverts and undermines the dominant patriarchal power of Jesus' day – the kingdom of Caesar. The kingdom of God is simply what the world would look like if God, not Caesar, ruled.[2] The metaphor suggests an ethic that reverses cultural norms: the last are first and the first last; the *poor* are lifted up and the rich sent away empty; the persecuted are blessed; rulers are servants; the well-being of the soul, not the size of one's bank account, defines the person; true wealth consists not in accumulating money but in allocating it; spiritual wisdom, not political power, is the hidden treasure; the humble, not the high and mighty, have access to wisdom; non-violence, not redemptive violence, is God's way. God's kingdom makes for a topsy-turvy life.

Furthermore, the early church announced that the title of God's "Son" belonged to a Jewish peasant nobody from the backwater of Galilee, and not to Caesar as Caesar claimed! Likewise, they subversively claimed that Jesus was the "Son of God," not Caesar. This title did not originally have the triumphalistic meaning that got attached to it later, as a way of distinguishing "true believers" from "infidels." Originally, it was intended to support a spiritual community who wanted to live out an alternative set of values than those upon which Caesar's kingdom was built.

We shouldn't be too hasty about tossing out these ancient metaphors. When understood in context, they are still subversive, and suggest that the core values of the Christian faith rarely line up easily with the core values of our dominant institutions. When those values are manipulated so that they do line up, clergy rush to the White House at times of war to pray for the President, or to prayer breakfasts of transnational corporations to lend an air of respectability to the occasion. There's nothing inherently wrong with showing up at either; God knows that at times of war we all need prayer. But let us do so remembering the subversive origins of the

Spirit movement of Jesus of Nazareth. The metaphor of the kingdom of God also invites us to ask subversive questions, such as why clergy are invited to the table *after* the troops have been deployed, but excluded from the discernment process that led to war in the first place.

My point is that the kingdom of God was a non-negotiable for Jesus. All other forms and structures were up for grabs. One of the first items of business for our Think Tank was to discern what our own non-negotiable elements would be. (This conversation helps to ease any change anxiety that surfaces in the group.)

Remember: when our Think Tank got together, we entered into a covenant that put every *form* on the line. There would be no sacred jars of purification. But there are *functional*, non-negotiable elements of an emergent church, and this group will find it helpful to discuss these. These non-negotiables represent the very foundation of our life as a congregation. Our Think Tank at Canadian Memorial spent weeks meeting to discern and to discuss what we would consider non-negotiable for our congregation. We settled on the following elements.

THE GOSPEL

The root meaning of the word *gospel* is "good news," or news of natural goodness. You may not be surprised to discover that this, too, was an intentionally subversive metaphor. All over the empire, through art, inscriptions, and all manner of proclamation, Caesar signalled the "good news" (the gospel) of his benevolent reign, sanctioned by the gods for the good of all the people. Well, Jesus had his own brand of good news, and it wasn't what Caesar had in mind.

There are two aspects to the gospel: first, what Jesus himself taught about the kingdom of God; and second, what the early church taught *about* Jesus and about the meaning of his life, death, and resurrection. Both are found in the writings we call the New Testament.

Unfortunately, none of this comes to us unfiltered. Both Jesus' own teaching and the teaching of the early church about him are presented and seen through the particular concerns and worldviews of the gospel writers and the communities for which they were writing. Sorting out what belongs to Jesus and what belongs to the early Christian communities need not be a threatening task. Sometimes the way the gospel writers interpret Jesus' teachings reflects their own fear of the radical nature of those teachings. At other times, it seems as though they may have simply misunderstood. And sometimes, their interpretations are brilliant. An emergent congregation accepts the truth that its take on reality, including the gospel, is inevitably partial. We'll never gain absolute clarity about the gospel. But as we wrestle with what has been passed down to us in the New Testament, and through that "great cloud of witnesses" in our tradition, our lives may be transformed.

You might think that the importance of the gospel is self-evident. However, I know of "progressive" congregations that read Shakespeare or other inspirational writings in worship, rather than wrestle with Jesus of Nazareth and the good news. I love poetry, essays, and various writings that are spiritually uplifting. They can even be revelatory. And there are many spiritual communities that serve the evolutionary purposes of the universe well by using these other forms of spiritual writing. But to be Christian is to set oneself and one's community in an ongoing dialogue with Jesus and his teachings. For us, this was a non-negotiable.

THE WHOLE BIBLE

Expanding out from the good news of the New Testament, our Think Tank thought that it was essential to affirm that the whole Bible, including the Old Testament or First Testament, is central to our identity as a congregation.

Many people prefer to just skip over the First Testament and get to the New Testament. Usually, their complaint focuses on the amount of violence in the First Testament, and on the sobering reality that a good bit of that violence is either purportedly sanctioned or executed by God. But remember, the Bible itself is a library of books that has been subject to an evolutionary process. The models of God, and the statements about God's purposes it contains, shift over time according to the evolving consciousness of the writers. And notice this: we also find the roots of *non-violence* in the First Testament. For example, the prophet Micah prophesies the time when swords will be turned into ploughshares (Micah 4:3). Truly, nothing Jesus teaches is absolutely unique to him. You can find it all in latent or explicit form in Jesus' own Bible – the Hebrew scriptures, or the Old or First Testament. What *is* unique is the way that Jesus synthesized, embodied, and then put his life on the line for the essential values in his tradition.

This should be good enough reason for us to want to know what's in this collection of songs, history, poetry, wisdom literature, and myth. Jesus' own mission statement (Luke 4) comes from Isaiah, one of the books in the First Testament. It's not possible to understand Jesus' teachings without knowing the core narratives of the First Testament. The writers of the gospels use them as a template to write the story of Jesus' life. At Canadian Memorial, therefore, we have chosen to resist any temptation to only read the New Testament.

New Testament scholar Marcus Borg says that the emerging church takes the Bible seriously, but not literally. If we are going to take the Bible seriously, Bible study must be an important part of the program. In my opinion, mainline churches are too complacent about teaching biblical literacy. As Christians, we have a sacred story that is the context of our own life stories, and we need to learn it. At Canadian Memorial, Bible study has become foundational. We teach a 34-week program and two nine-week modules that are primarily focused on content – what's *in* the Bible. We also teach a continuous study in six-week modules that focuses more on personal transformation. Participants learn to read the stories metaphorically. In my experience, most mainline church members have never learned to read scripture in this way. For example, when Jesus asks the disciples to "push out into deeper waters and let down their nets," a metaphorical question might be, "Where in our lives right now are we being asked to push out into deeper waters?" Learning to read the Bible metaphorically is part of what it means to be biblically literate. When the stories of our faith intersect with the stories of our lives there can be an explosion of meaning. The Holy One, to whom all of the stories point, shines through the pages.

New people who show up at church – especially younger people – are likely to know next to nothing about scripture. Often, they are self-conscious about their lack of knowledge. This self-consciousness may be even stronger in people who have attended church for a long time, but who feel that their biblical knowledge may still be inadequate. It's important not underestimate how intimidated either group of people may feel. At Canadian Memorial, we have found it helpful, when introducing our Bible studies, to make it absolutely clear that no prior knowledge of scripture is required.

AN OPEN TABLE

Our Think Tank also decided that, for us, the sacrament of the open table – the Eucharist or Communion – is a non-negotiable. Following in the Wisdom tradition of his own faith, Jesus acted as a "child of Wisdom." One of the primary activities of Sophia (Wisdom) was to prepare a banquet to which all the "simple" (foolish) ones were invited. The purpose of the feast was to transform their foolish ways with her primordial wisdom (Proverbs 9:1–5).

Following in this tradition, Jesus was known for his own "banquets." He gained a reputation for being a "drunkard and a sinner" because he enjoyed organizing these dinners. John Dominic Crossan sees Jesus' table ministry as his primary way of enacting the kingdom of God.[3] These table gatherings subverted Caesar's rule, the way of power as domination, as another ethic emerged – the way of love, compassion, and inclusivity.

It was natural for Jesus' followers to remember him following his death, by gathering around a table to share food. Jesus shared these meals with the "pure" and the "impure," and with people of different class systems. His intent was to break down the social walls that divide. Sinners and saints would sup together to receive nourishment for the body and spiritual wisdom for the soul. Today we call this symbolic meal Communion, the Eucharist, or the Lord's Supper, depending on our tradition. There are three primary ways of understanding the meal.

Mystical

Many people believe that they are taking the very essence of Christ (the body and the blood) into their own being as they share the symbolic meal of bread and wine. They are receiving the spiritual power of Christ's presence. This gives them the capacity to be a Christ-like presence in the world.

Eschatological – End Times

Others see the ritual meal as a symbolic representation of where we are headed as God's people. With everyone welcome at the table, the radically inclusive nature of God's future is present. It is a foretaste of the ultimate realization of our unity – with God, with all humanity, and with the planet along with all her creatures. We experience in the present God's intended future.

Common Meal

Others experience it as a symbolic meal, plain and simple. The table is a table, much like our own kitchen tables, around which the family gathers to share news of the day and to be nourished. They see the meal as the church's way of signalling to itself and to the community that we live in a world in which two-thirds of humanity is physically hungry, and in which we have created false divisions – disparities in wealth; access to clean food, water, and health care; gender injustice, religious divisions, and many more. By ritually re-enacting this meal in the name of Christ, we take up Christ's mission to heal these divisions.

Running through all these ways of understanding this sacred meal is gratitude for Jesus' own self-donation in the service of abundant life, justice, and lasting peace. In a creation-centred paradigm, the ritual of the broken bread and the shared cup is not a re-enactment of a blood sacrifice required by God on our behalf. The table is a table, not an altar upon which we re-enact this sacrifice.

At best, all three of these meanings are active. We *do* tap into the soul of Christ, receiving wisdom and power to be the body of Christ. Communion *is* an experience of the future present, when false divisions and the coercive exercise of power give way to an ethic of love. At the same time, it is a simple meal, at which the hungry are fed and the spiritually hungry receive wisdom for the journey. Through it all, we give thanks that Jesus held nothing back, not even his life, but offered himself in the service of our healing.

Crucial in all three understandings is that the table is *open to all.* My wife, Ann, and I went to Israel on a study tour for three weeks. The tour group included men and women from across the entire Christian spectrum of denominations. Over the three weeks, we came to know each other deeply. Near the end of our time together, in Jesus' home province of Galilee, a communion service was arranged. You can imagine the anticipation we all felt, sharing this sacred meal where Jesus walked and taught. When it came time to distribute the bread and the wine, the presider announced that if we were not part of his particular denomination we couldn't participate. We were flabbergasted, crushed, and angry. In Jesus' name and in his own province, we were excluded!

When I issue the invitation to receive the bread and wine, I make a point of saying something like, "This is not our table. It is Christ's table. Therefore, all are welcome at it. You don't have to be a member of our congregation. You don't have to believe what we believe. It's not about believing the 'right' things. This is a banquet of love, where false divisions between 'us' and 'them' are dissolved in the name and presence of Christ. You are welcome at this table, friends."

Every time we offer Communion, at least one newcomer tells me how much it meant to them to be included. Remember, visitors don't know they are welcome unless we tell them. They don't know the secret code and they assume, believe me, that there is one. Their radar is on red alert for signs that they aren't really welcome.

In the congregation I serve, we attract progressive Buddhists, Sikhs, Muslims, and New Age seekers, even atheists who simply feel loved and who want more of it. A-theism literally means to not believe in a theistic God, one who lives outside the cosmos, but who intervenes every once in a while to sort us out. I don't believe in that kind of God either. These souls who attend Canadian Memorial (typically 25–45 years of age) experience a radical hospitality. It's part of the culture we've felt called to create. They see absolutely no problem being Buddhist and Christian, or Sikh and Christian. It will be interesting to see how this postmodern phenomenon shapes the church of the 21st century.

The radically inclusive ethic of Christ in the 21st century, expressed in the open table, is creating new forms, new understandings of what it means to be "in Christ." Honestly, I don't know what to make of it yet. But I know this much: it is part and parcel of the emerging church. When we welcome these hybrid saints we are not being altogether altruistic. There is an enlightened self-interest at work. Whatever it is they are getting from being with us, we are receiving as much from them. This exchange represents the emergent principle of novelty in action. They are an integral part of our emerging future, the new thing God is doing in our midst. Could it be that they will influence us to broaden our understanding of the nature of Christ, a nature that is planetary in scope, encompassing all people of every faith and of no faith?

DISCIPLESHIP

Christians are disciples of Christ, not members of a church club. Members pay their dues and want to know what they are getting for their money. Disciples make an offering of all their resources and want to know how their money is being used for Christ. Members expect a regular visit from their minister – after all, they're card-carrying members! Disciples expect to visit the sick, the imprisoned, and the lonely. Members help "the minister" out. Disciples discern and deploy their *own* gifts for ministry. Members focus on institutional maintenance. Disciples focus on mission. Members fill bureaucratic slots in the church system. Disciples serve according to their Spirit-given gifts. Members have an organizational affiliation. They talk about how many years they have been members. Disciples express their allegiance to Christ in a dynamic faith community and want to talk about the difference their community of faith is making in the world.[4]

When I started out in ministry, 1,700 years of Christendom (when to be a citizen of the mainstream culture was by default to be Christian) had taken the edge off the meaning of discipleship. In my first ten years of ministry, I felt something was missing. Congregations seemed to lack a clear identity. Individuals were reluctant to claim an identity as a disciple of Christ. It seemed to me that, like many other symbols and metaphors, the mainline church had ceded the identity of "disciple" to evangelical and fundamentalist Christians. Our Think Tank wanted to reclaim this core metaphor and identity.

In Canada, the dominant culture is decidedly not Christian. Most people regard themselves as spiritual. They believe in a "higher power," but distance themselves from any institutional expression of this belief. They are "spiritual" not "religious." But the distinction is overly simplistic. Any New Age spirituality that intends to be around for more than a decade or so is going to have to get organized. The problem is not with "institutional" religion. The problem lies with religious institutions that don't embrace an emergent principle and therefore never evolve.

Today, we have a great opportunity, similar in many ways to the opportunity the early church had. In Canada, Christians are a fringe element in society. We have the opportunity to experience the difference between a membership paradigm and a discipleship paradigm. Discipleship means "disciplined spiritual growth." We know that we cannot expect to keep our physical bodies in good condition without going to the gym, walking briskly on a daily basis, watching what we eat, and stretching our muscles. It's no different when it comes to attending to the life of the Spirit. Our life in Christ requires attention. Thus, we regularly celebrate God's presence in worship, give generously and regularly of our financial abundance and of our Spirit-given gifts, take time for prayer, keep the Sabbath, care for the earth, and make justice a reality. These aren't meant to be a burden. These are the joyful fruits of life in Christ, a *response* to the grace of God, not the *means* by which we attain it.

A colleague of mine introduced his congregation to this discipleship paradigm much to the chagrin and resistance of many of the "members." When he met with them they were direct: "All of this discipleship talk is ruining our church. We want it back the way it was before." There was absolutely nothing wrong with what they wanted. They just didn't want the church. They wanted Club Christendom back. Many left the congregation. It wasn't the end of the world, however. It was the beginning of a great adventure with those who yearned for a disciplined life of the Spirit. In her book *Christianity for the Rest of Us*, Diana Butler Bass talks about the "intentional" church – congregations that offer intentional spiritual practice as the very heart of their common life.[5] These are the congregations that are thriving.

MISSION AND JUSTICE

The final non-negotiable our Think Tank team identified was mission. Many people still associate mission with sending missionaries overseas to developing nations. This is certainly one form of mission. But if you want to know where the mission field is in the 21st century, look out at your congregation on any Sunday morning. Or poke your head out the door of the sanctuary and take a look around your neighbourhood.

Let me be perfectly clear about what our team did *not* mean by mission. We did not mean "bringing souls to Jesus." For us, mission is more about bringing Jesus to hungry souls and hungry bodies, not to convert them, but because they are hungry and Jesus calls us to feed them. Many of those hungry souls will naturally want to become part of the Body of Christ and we need to be intentional about helping them with a life of discipleship. But we don't do mission to put bums in seats or to save souls for "eternal life."

In his song *This Thing in My Heart*, Bruce Cockburn writes, "I've got this thing in my heart, I must give you today. It only lives when you give it away." The thing is love, and the only way to keep it alive is to find ways to give it away. Nothing defines a healthy congregation better than how much love they give away. When a congregation "gets it" that it's not about them – not about meeting the budget, or providing programs for members, or making sure they all get a visit from the minister or that the minister is meeting the needs of the members – its chances of survival increase exponentially.

The Very Reverend David Giuliano, Moderator of the United Church of Canada, says about mission,

> I am praying that more of us become concerned with Jesus' call to feed the hungry, clothe the naked, and shelter the homeless…
> I am praying that our preoccupation with getting people into church is transformed by a passion for getting the church into the world. I am praying that we welcome strangers with a radical hospitality that sees in them the face of Christ – not an "identifiable giver" or a "potential committee member"! I am praying that our worries about buildings and budgets are overtaken by excitement for the mission of the church.[6]

Newcomers arrive at a church with a set of assumptions (many of them mistaken) about church life – that we're morally superior, or we're a conflict-free zone, or that we're all biblical scholars. But one assumption they are not wrong about is that we should be about serving a purpose that transcends our own survival. Many church models place mission at the end of a long process of initiation. Mission consciousness is said to kick in only after we mature as Christians. That's not my experience. The once-a-month dinner that we serve in the inner city is an *entry-point* into the community, not the end-point of the initiation of those who serve the meal. The people who make this ministry happen assume that this is what churches do – feed the hungry, reach out to the poor, make peace in the community – and their intuition is right on the money.

Mission, biblical literacy, an open table, proclaiming the gospel, and discipleship – these became our non-negotiables, the scaffolding upon which the new thing God is doing may emerge, the very heart and mind of Christ at Canadian Memorial. I recommend that your team discern and articulate your own non-negotiables. The forms we create – the jars, to return to the metaphor from Chapter 2 – will serve these ends.

MAPPING IT OUT

1. Get buy-in from your existing core leaders. Your lead ministers, including your minister of music, and the board (or council or elders) must be ready, willing, and able to commit to this journey of culture shifting. Don't kid yourself. This process of intentional culture shifting will be tough. Without commitment from your core leaders, you won't have the staying power.

2. Form a leadership team – a group we called the Think Tank. You need the right people in the right places. We handpicked this team. There are other ways, of course, but don't rule this way out.

3. Have the Think Tank enter into a change covenant. Put all structures on the line. Everything is on the table for change, except your non-negotiables. At a service of worship, have a covenanting service with the congregation to bless this team. Receiving the blessing and support of the congregation at this point is crucial.

4. Deal with the fear-factor by talking about how nature adapts, transcends, and includes, and about how wholes become parts of larger wholes.

5. Work on your "non-negotiables." Structures may come and go, but there are certain functions without which the church ceases to be a church. These non-negotiables are the very heart and mind of Christ and will be tested later in the process by taking them to the congregation.

6. Teach the leadership team about emergent processes in nature. Gather stories about congregations that have made culture shifts. Read books on congregational renewal. You are creating your own microclimate for change in this group.

7. Consider taking the team to congregations that have been through an intentional culture-shifting process. We flew our team to a church in Calgary, Alberta, and visited an evangelical church in Bellingham, Washington. We spent time listening to their stories of how they managed change, and the difference it has made to the life of the congregation. These visits were pivotal.

8. Remember, while the transition may be tough, it is a high and holy calling. By the power of the Spirit, you and your team can do this. The time is now.

[1] Ronald Rolheisser, *The Holy Longing: A Search for a Christian Spirituality* (New York: Doubleday, 1999), 45.

[2] John Dominic Crossan, *Jesus: A Revolutionary Biography* (San Francisco: HarperSanFrancisco, 1994), 54ff.

[3] John Dominic Crossan, *The Historical Jesus: The Life of a Mediterranean Jewish Peasant* (New York, HarperCollins Publishers, 1992,) 341.

[4] I want to acknowledge the contribution of Michael W. Foss to naming this shift from membership to discipleship, in particular, his book *Power Surge: Six Marks of Discipleship for a Changing Church* (Minneapolis: Fortress Press, 2000), 11ff.

[5] Diana Butler Bass, *Christianity for the Rest of Us: How the Neighborhood Church Is Transforming the Faith* (San Francisco: HarperSanFrancisco, 2006). The whole book is filled with examples of discipleship programs.

[6] The Very Reverend David Giuliano, *The Moderator's Message*, October, 2007.

four

The Body of Christ: Vision and Mission

Now you are the body of Christ and individually members of it.
~ 1 CORINTHIANS 12:27 ~

Articulating your congregation's non-negotiables is the beginning of a process of *self-definition*. Self-definition is a built-in feature of the universe, manifesting in galaxies, solar systems, cells, organisms, and all living systems. In the human realm, individuals and organizations enjoy the capacity for *conscious* self-definition. Every individual and every community functions optimally as a centre of creative emergence only by clearly defining itself – what it is and what it is not. *Self-expression flows from clear self-definition.* If you lack clarity about your parameters and purposes, you will lack power and presence when it comes to self-expression.

After articulating the congregation's non-negotiables, the next step in congregational self-definition is articulating a vision and mission statement.

At Canadian Memorial, the Board gave the Think Tank an explicit mandate to develop a new organizational model, a way of governing that would reflect an emergent culture. We wanted the new thing that God is doing in the world and in our congregation to manifest from the inside out, in and through the Body of Christ. At the same time, we wanted to enable the members of our congregation to express their unique sense of calling, and we wanted to establish this creative self-expression as a norm. This was the "deliverable," what we intended to birth.

To accomplish this, we had to begin by asking ourselves what we were organizing *for*. We needed to discern our function before we could determine the forms that would embody them: ministry teams, small groups, educational programs, worship style… In doing so, we were aligning ourselves with nature's way. The particular form an organism or a system takes in nature invariably arises simultaneously with its function in an ecosystem.

Discovering a congregation's purpose is not as obvious or straightforward a task as it might seem and requires a lot of discernment. If the congregation is still living with a hangover from the age of Christendom, it's that much more difficult. As discussed earlier, for many congregations, their purpose is about membership in Club Christendom and not about discipleship. Furthermore, in an emergent model, each congregation will manifest their own distinctive culture, what the corporate world calls their "brand." In order to arrive at this unique expression, the congregation needs to define their vision and mission.

Mention to your congregation that you want to develop a vision and mission statement and there's a good chance your announcement will be met by groans and sighs too deep for words. Many people are cynical about this kind of exercise, and justifiably so. To the extent that vision and mission statements simply reflect a wish list, or some pie-in-the-sky vision disconnected from the actual life of the congregation, they are next to useless.

To make matters worse, many congregations simply import a process that members may have gone through at work. Too often, these are top-down exercises, written by a wordsmith executive and then distributed down the line. It doesn't matter how well-crafted these statements are, how fancy the calligraphy and framing is, or how many walls you hang them on. If the people who will be living the statement out weren't involved in its development, it will remain nothing more than an inert document that will not galvanize the energy of the congregation.

Unfortunately, the opposite approach creates its own set of problems. It's possible to have too much involvement by too many people. By the time many vision and mission statements get to their final form, they are so watered down by a genuine attempt to honour everyone's input that they are neither inspiring nor particularly useful. The scope of many statements is so broad that they will never function as the practical tool they are meant to be. Vision and mission statements are meant to be functional.

GOOD IDEAS VERSUS GOVERNING IDEAS[1]

There is a difference between good ideas and governing ideas. Good ideas are a dime a dozen. Vision and mission statements express governing ideas. They shape faith formation programs, Sunday school curricula, and mission projects. Your website design, newsletter formats, and priority policies around which your minister and lay ministry teams operate will express these statements. Governing ideas define the congregation – your purpose, what you're going to do, the difference you hope to make in the world, and for whom.[2]

JESUS' VISION AND MISSION

A mission statement describes the purpose of the congregation. I'll deal with this in more detail below. A vision statement is a compelling image or description of the difference you intend to make by being faithful to that purpose. Let's start with Jesus' own vision. One day at synagogue, acting as the lay reader and preacher, he picks up the scroll of the prophet Isaiah and reads:

The Spirit of the Lord is upon me,

because he has anointed me to bring good news to the poor.

> He has sent me to proclaim release to the captives
> and recovery of sight to the blind,
> to let the oppressed go free,
> to proclaim the year of the Lord's favour (Luke 4:18–19).

The key comes in what he says after the reading. Jesus sits down to preach, as was the custom, then makes an astonishing claim: "Today this scripture has been fulfilled in your hearing" (4:21). Jesus publicly declares that he intends to embody this vision. The Spirit has sent *him,* personally, to declare that a new age has dawned, one that lifts the nobodies and nuisances out of the dust of empire and liberates them to share in the abundant life of the Spirit. If you are looking for an example of a person who is Spirit filled, anointed, liberated, and willing to speak out, look no further than me, Jesus tells his followers. He is both the walk and the talk. He *is* the future that he proclaims. He's not going to merely act upon the world – he intends to act *as* the new world he envisions. The past, present, and future coalesce in him.

A vision is only as effective as a congregation's willingness to actually embody it. A church becomes the Body of Christ – manifesting the heart and mind of Christ – when the vision lights them up from within. This is the inner radiance we are looking for. The public should be able to look at your congregation and see your vision alive and well in the world. No one said it would be easy.

Notice, Jesus is clear about his constituency – the poor, the blind, and the oppressed. He's not going to spend a lot of time trying to convince Caesar, his minions, or the aristocracy that *they* should change. Rather, he's going to go directly to the left-behinds of the world to empower them to enter and then co-create God's kingdom and thereby exit Caesar's. His audience comes from a culture that he is familiar with. As a Jewish peasant, he knows what it's like to have the boot of Rome firmly planted on his neck. These are his people. He knows them intimately.

Jesus is also clear about the *difference he intends to make in the world*. Captives are released, the blind see, the oppressed are liberated, and the year of the Lord's favour, or the year of Jubilee, is proclaimed. So it's clear *who* Jesus' constituency is, and the *difference* his vision will make in their lives. These are the components of an effective vision.

JESUS' MISSION — THE KINGDOM OF GOD

This vision of the difference Jesus intended to make through his movement was captured in a core metaphor that became his mission – to proclaim and enact the kingdom of God. You won't find the kingdom on a map, nor is it the place where the faithful go to receive their heavenly reward. It is life, here and now, lived in right relationship to God, self, others, and today we would add the earth.

We could learn a thing or two about our own mission statements by noticing a few things about Jesus' mission.

First, it's succinct, and therefore memorable: "Proclaim and enact the kingdom of God." Immediately, I'm curious. I want to know more. You could recite it in a heartbeat if anybody asked. Rambling mission statements signal a lack of clarity about the purpose of a congregation or organization.

Second, it is an oppositional and subversive metaphor. If I enter God's kingdom, then by definition I exit Caesar's. It redefines the conventional understanding of kingdom. Nevertheless, it is positively stated. There's a difference between taking a position and taking a stand. We take a position *against* something, but we stand *for* a cause. The brilliance of Jesus' mission is that in taking a stand *for* the kingdom of God, he implicitly undermines the authority of Caesar's kingdom. But notice: he didn't waste a lot of time opposing Caesar's kingdom directly. Caesar's kingdom was undermined by a withdrawal of allegiance to it, not by attacking it. Jesus was actively building a new reality, not simply deconstructing an old one. This was Gandhi's strategy as well. And also the strategy used by Martin Luther King Jr. When Martin Luther King

Jr. stood up to deliver his most famous speech, he did not say, "I have a complaint." No, he said, "I have a dream." To be sure, that dream of equality, and of equal access to education, and of opportunity for African Americans, threatened the status quo, but it described what he stood for, not merely what he was against.

We in the mainline churches could spend a little less time telling everybody within earshot what we're against, and a little more energy building the kind of world we stand for. I know. We call it prophetic ministry – speaking truth to power. And it's important to have the courage to do this. But if we spend more time speaking out *against* the status quo than speaking *for* the new dream, it drains the energy from our people. I've been guilty of this myself, but now I'm realizing how much more difficult it is to actually do what Jesus did, to go out and create an alternative reality and inspire others to pitch in. We need to articulate the kind of world we intend to build, in the name of Christ, and then equip our people with hammers and nails, and inspire them to build it, one life at a time.

Finally, Jesus' mission statement is comprehensive: proclaim and enact the kingdom of God. While it is succinct, it is also paradoxically vast. The kingdom of God encompasses all realms of existence: personal, social, political, economic, and religious, with its positively stated but implicitly subversive intent. Here's a chart that captures how this single metaphor offers an alternative model of reality on five different levels at once.

	KINGDOM OF CAESAR	KINGDOM OF GOD
Personal	I am a servant of Caesar.	I am a disciple of Christ, serving God and humanity.
Social	I am born into a social rank and am valued accordingly	I am a child of God, which alone confers my worth.

Political	I have no voice.	My voice deserves to be heard.
Economic	I am a cog in Caesar's economic machinery. Wealth is money.	My work serves God. Wealth is the quality of my relationships.
Religious	Caesar is my god. Money is his currency.	There is only one God. Love is God's only currency.

To really "get" the kingdom of God, in other words, is to undergo a radical transformation that reorients one's entire life. When we discover our mission – our purpose as a congregation – it makes us want to roll up our sleeves and dig in. In the 12th century, Thomas Aquinas said that humans are *capax universi*, capable of the universe. Our souls long to be involved in a mission that is alluring – in other words it lights us up from the inside out and calls to us as a project worthy of our soul's grandness.

THE KIN-DOM OF GOD – A MISSION FOR THE 21ST CENTURY

A mission statement, then, is a broad statement of purpose, a public declaration of why we exist as a congregation in the first place. If followed, it will inspire us to create a new life and co-create a new world – one that is aligned with God's intentions for life on this planet. Following Jesus' example, it will be succinct, memorable, positively stated, and comprehensive – worthy of the grandness of our souls.

A congregation in the 21st century could do worse than to drop the "g" in kingdom, and have a mission statement that simply read, "We proclaim and enact the kin-dom of God." While we no longer have to contend with kings or queens set on conquering "new worlds," world leaders continue to exhibit an instinct to dominate, if not in an explicitly political way, then certainly economically. In the last decade, the U.S. administration has enacted an explicitly neo-imperial foreign policy. Furthermore, human beings are in the process of colonizing the entire planet, destroying the natural habitat of plants and animals at an unprecedented rate. This ethic of domination is made possible because we deny our kinship with all of life. When we do not feel the radical interconnectedness of life, we enact terror upon the planet. The kin-dom of God subverts not only political and economic forms of domination, but also the ecological colonization of the planet by humans.

We live in an era of hyper-individualism ill suited to the continuation of life on the planet Earth.[3] Living by the logic of ego, as though we're all isolated beings or lone corporations in competition with each other, is killing us. We need to replace ego-logic with eco-logic. We now know that we're embedded in interdependent ecosystems, both natural and cultural. While there is differentiation within these systems, there is no disconnection – anywhere. We also know that in an evolutionary universe we all derive from common stock and therefore we are cosmologically, biologically, and culturally related – kin with all of life. Kinship is not an abstract ideal in the universe we share. It is a fundamental truth. Imagine a community of faith dedicating itself to living out of this identity in contrast to a culture of hyper-individualism.

	HYPER-INDIVIDUALISM	KIN-DOM OF GOD
Personal	I am an isolated being, forging a path in a hostile competitive world.	I belong to a community of beings, cooperatively creating a future fit for life.
Social	I am what I make of myself.	I am a composite of all the beings that preceded me, and of all my relationships.
Economic	Economics is money.	Economics is *oikonomos* – care of my personal and planetary home.

Political	I vote for whoever can make my own life easier.	I vote for whoever represents the interests of the whole ecosystem, human and other-than-human.
Religious	My personal salvation is my primary concern.	The healing of all creation, including humans, is my concern.

Here's a possible vision and mission statement inspired by the gospel story, but updated for the 21st century.

Mission

We proclaim and enact God's kin-dom:

 the family of God that is the sacred community of life,

  where all belong,

   everything is connected,

    and every being is cherished.

Vision

The Spirit of God is upon us so that

- We embody the kin-dom in our personal lives and in our relationships with each other as a community of faith.
- We hear and honour the voiceless ones, both human and other-than-human.
- The planet is made whole again: the trees clap their hands, the mountains rejoice, and the waters sing.

To reiterate, the mission is a statement of purpose and the vision is an image or description of the difference we intend to make in the world, and for whom, if we are living in alignment with this purpose.

 Notice one other thing: Jesus doesn't feel the need to re-create the wheel. The kingdom of God was a metaphor in circulation in his day.

He did, however, change the meaning from a geographical location that a Messiah should be prepared to fight for, to a non-violent way of being in the world that one entered through the practice of spiritual wisdom. This new spin on a familiar metaphor captured the imagination of his followers. The same is true for his vision. It came right out of his scriptural tradition. But again, it moved him personally and therefore had the potential of moving others. The point is, we may borrow from existing visions, as long as they light us up from within.

GIVE IT TO ME, STRAIGHT FROM THE HEART

We have three major neural systems in the human body, located in the brain, the heart, and the intestinal track. Too often, our mission and vision statements come solely *from* the brain and are therefore directed *to* the brain of others. But our mission and vision must reach the gut and the heart, not just the head, if it is going to galvanize your congregation's energy. Physicist Henri Bortoft distinguishes the "counterfeit whole," a purely intellectual take on reality, from the "authentic whole," one that senses reality with the heart and the gut as well as the head. A vision and mission statement must capture that authentic whole, the heart and mind of Christ manifest in your congregation. It must tap into the soul of your life together as a community of faith.

Bortoft goes on to say that "a part is a place for the presencing of the whole."[4] If we take the "part" to be the congregational member, our hope is that she begins to so identify with the vision and mission of the congregation that she takes responsibility for manifesting it, which is really what discipleship is all about. She is the part that embodies the whole. For her, the vision and mission are not abstract statements that exist outside herself. Rather, they describe a living system, the Body of Christ, of which she is a part – a part through whom the whole, the Christ, is born.

This describes perfectly what happened through Jesus that day in the synagogue. He read the passage from Isaiah and concluded that this was written *for* him and would manifest *through* him. "In your hearing this reading has been fulfilled" (Luke 4:21).

ONE MORE ACTION STEP

There is one more step involved in translating the vision and mission into action. In the governance model I present in Chapter 12, it is the Board's role to develop and articulate "ends statements" and "priority policies," which will be based on the vision and mission statements. These will clearly define in measurable terms the differences the congregation is making – in other words, how the vision and mission is being translated into action. Using the vision statement above as an example, the priority policy related to the vision of the repair of the planet might include, "The minister will ensure that at least two major ecological initiatives are taken by the congregation, one of which will involve our children," and/or "The minister will ensure that an ecological audit by an independent professional company of our facilities and operations will be carried out annually." The priority policy related to the vision of giving voice to the voiceless might include, "The minister will ensure that the congregation is given the opportunity to participate in ecumenical initiatives related to homelessness in Vancouver." The priority policy related to being the kin-dom of God with each other might include, "The minister will promote and develop *Be the Change* groups in the congregation." The minister will be held accountable for creating the systems and the culture by which the congregation may achieve these ends. But remember: these priorities are established by the Board, and are approved by the congregation, so there is an implicit shared responsibility. This ensures that the vision and mission statement is not merely decorative.

MAPPING IT OUT

1. Engage in a World Café process with your congregation.[5] This is a groundbreaking way to get to the heart of the congregation. At a congregational retreat called to kick-start the process of defining the vision and mission, set up a room to look like a café. For tablecloths use large pieces of flipchart paper. Have crayons, pens, and pencils at each table. Participants are going to be involved in a "conversation that matters." Ask your Think Tank team to spend some time, prior to the retreat, developing guiding questions to help the conversation go deep: questions such as,

   a. What is the future that needs me/our congregation in order to be born? (Martin Buber)

   b. What is it about this community that makes your heart sing?

   c. What hymn, or popular song, captures the essence of this community for you and why?

   d. What would the larger community miss about us if we ceased to exist?

   e. If this congregation were an animal, what animal would we be?

   f. What is the deep need of the world in our neighbourhood?

   g. What is the one Bible story, parable, or scriptural teaching that "says it all"?

   h. What would it mean for our congregation to do our mission *for* Christ and *as* Christ's body?

Choose *one* of these questions or develop your own. The World Café process works as people move from table to table having multiple conversations focused *on the same question*. People draw images and write comments on the "tablecloths" that capture the conversation, and a table facilitator records key repeating themes.

Over the course of many conversations around the same question, a group-intelligence – as Christians, we might prefer to call it Wisdom – begins to manifest. The inner life of the congregation is connecting more deeply with itself and as this happens the life within the life of the congregation begins to manifest. What was background – the Wisdom of the Christ – becomes foreground. The presence of the heart and mind of Christ palpably fills the room. The saying attributed to Christ, "Where two or three are gathered in my name, there am I in their midst," speaks to the power of conversation. What do we think was happening when Christ walked through the closed doors to appear to the disciples in Jerusalem, after the crucifixion (John 20:19–23)? I suspect they were in meaningful conversation about their life in Christ when he dropped in on them. World Café conversations are one way to intentionally foster domains of creative emergence in your congregation.

At the end of the day, the results of these holy conversations are gathered up and reviewed by the Think Tank. This is the beginning, I repeat, *the beginning* of the vision and mission process, not the end. The participants need to know this. Lay out the process for them. Be as clear as possible that the vision and mission statement will be succinct, comprehensive, and memorable; it will describe the difference you will make in the world, and for whom. What it won't be is a laundry list of everything they came up with at the retreat. But it *will* resonate with the spirit of the conversation – or it won't be adopted. Assure the participants that their conversation will find its way to a trusted group of leaders, who will develop a draft statement. This statement will be brought back to the congregation for their input, and ultimately their approval.

2. Have someone who is gifted in writing and theological reflection draft a statement of the vision and mission of the congregation based on the results of the World Café conversation.

3. Give this statement to your leadership team/Think Tank for reflection, prayer, discernment, and editing.

4. Oh yes, and check your egos at the door before every meeting. Seriously. This is no time to be "nice" with each other. You are birthing the Christ. Be prepared to have your best efforts deconstructed at every turn.

5. After you have a drafted statement – and do write DRAFT all over the copy –develop a process to take it to the whole congregation. Make it crystal clear that the congregation is free to do with it as they choose, on a continuum from accepting it, tweaking it, or sending it back to the drawing board. People will be keenly interested to see whether the statement reflects the spirit of their conversation. Record their feedback carefully.

6. Check your egos once again.

7. Rewrite based on feedback. You may need to take it back to the congregation at this point. What's the rush?

8. Do a final draft to present at a congregational meeting for approval. At this point, it should be a slam-dunk decision and a mighty celebration. If you think it's going to be controversial, don't present it. You're not there yet.

[1] Peter Senge, et al., *Presence: An Exploration of Profound Change in People, Organizations, and Society* (New York: Doubleday, 2005), 169.
[2] John Carver, Miriam Carver, *Reinventing Your Board: A Step-by-Step Guide to Implementing Policy Governance* (San Francisco: Jossey-Bass, 1997).
[3] Bill McKibbon, *Deep Economy: The Wealth of Communities and the Durable Future* (New York: Henry Holt and Company, 2007), 96–98.
[4] Senge, *Presence*, 7.
[5] Juanita Brown and David Isaacs, *The World Café: Shaping Our Futures through Conversations that Matter* (San Francisco: Berrett-Koehler Publishers Inc., 2005).

five

From Church Spire to Spiral Dynamics: Value Systems and Congregational Life

For now I know only in part; then I will know fully…
~ 1 CORINTHIANS 13:12 ~

What I am proposing is that the psychology of the mature human being is an unfolding, emergent, oscillating, spiraling process, marked by progressive subordination of old, lower-order behavior systems to new, higher-order systems as man's existential problems change.
~ DR. CLARE GRAVES ~

Many congregations develop a values statement along with their vision and mission statement. These statements help newcomers get a read on the culture or ethos of a community. A newcomer can take a quick glance over a congregation's values statement and pretty much determine if this is a place that fits with their own values. For example, if you read Canadian Memorial's values statement (see Appendix 1) you'll discover that under "inclusivity" we do not discriminate based on sexual orientation, and we believe that all religious traditions have their own valid window on the Holy. One of our values, "innovation," says that we celebrate change, as the Spirit moves us. Reading this statement, a person with traditional values would quickly understand that should he decide to stay, he's making a decision to be stretched. The values statement is a thumbnail sketch of a congregation's culture.

For centuries, the church spire towered into the heavens. At best, the spire was a symbol of human yearning to be connected with the transcendent divine. At worst, it acted as a lightning rod conducting the revelation of God directly down to the pulpit, whereupon the preacher would deliver the unchanging, infallible truth. The true believer was the repository of a set of unchanging values, which would serve him or her for life.

It's possible now to articulate our organizational value systems within the context of a much more comprehensive understanding of cultural value systems or worldviews, which comes to us through the field of developmental psychology. The truth is that value systems evolve along with the rest of the universe. When it comes to value systems, the church spire is giving way to the spiral.

"There is a theory that history moves in cycles. But, like a spiral staircase, when the course of human events comes full circle it does so on a new level."[1] This spiral movement of history also occurs at the level of the human psyche and at the level of our foundational value systems, which shape our worldviews. The spiral is an archetypal symbol emerging out of natural processes. It is associated with both the energies of destruction and creation.

I once had a dream in which I was travelling on a bus with other passengers. I saw a tornado approaching and realized we were directly in its path. Indeed, the tornado picked the bus up and rolled it two or three times. Miraculously, nobody was hurt. I climbed out of a window and was met by a man who told me that I had been chosen to name a new species of tree. I knew absolutely nothing about trees and told him so, but to no avail. This was the task I had been given.

Interpreting the dream later, I realized that the spiral shape of the tornado was a sign that I was in the midst of a transformative process. I was being shaken up, challenged to make room for the emergent reality that was coming into my life. This is the way evolution happens, at both the personal and cultural levels.

The spiral is a fractal form, a natural structure that repeats itself at a micro level and at a macro level. The double helix spiral of the DNA molecule is a micro expression, while the spiral structures of some galaxies reflect the macro phase of the fractal. You see a fractal forms in nature because it works so well. Through natural processes, Spirit very efficiently carries forward what works. For the purposes of evolution, this means that the spiral is a fractal structure associated with emergence, the creative dynamic by which new forms transcend yet include previous forms.

The late Dr. Clare W. Graves, a pioneer in the field of developmental psychology, noticed that worldviews and value systems evolved in a developmental fashion. As new challenges and life conditions confront a culture, new worldviews and value systems emerge in order to help the culture adapt and evolve. It turns out that human societies, not just biological life systems, also "escape to a higher order" (a process discussed in Chapter 1). This doesn't happen so much in a linear fashion, Graves theorized, but rather like a spiral staircase that circles back on itself. With each revolution, these new value systems or worldviews ascend, reaching a higher level in an effort to resolve the challenges created by the previous stage.

Graves called his model Spiral Dynamics. Don Beck colour-coded these levels for the layperson's benefit, since Grave's original typology is a bit awkward. Below is a brief description of the colours, the associated value systems, and the life conditions that give rise to them. I am indebted to the brilliant work of Dr. Don Beck, a student of Clare Graves, who has dedicated his life to teaching this system.[2]

STAGES OF SPIRAL DYNAMICS

(See colour insert.
Also available to download at www.woodlakebooks.com/emergingchurch)

BEIGE: Archaic/Survivalist Value System (emerged 100,000 years ago)

When the two-legged ones stood up and ventured out into the savannahs of Africa, it was a case of eat or be eaten. Life for humans, along with the rest of the animals, boiled down to a search for water, food, and shelter. They travelled in bands because it was safer than travelling alone as an individual. Yet each individual within the band looked out for his or her own interests. You can see the survival instinct up close and personal in infants at the first sign of hunger or discomfort.

Congregations have been known to regress to this level under financial duress! When we find ourselves hunkering down and focusing exclusively on survival, we are operating from a survivalist value system.

PURPLE: Tribal Value System (emerged 50,000 years ago)

Clans bump into each other and begin to form more complex tribal systems. Out of the primarily individualistic instinct for survival, loyalty to the tribe and to the ancestors issues in a more communitarian value system. At this stage, the whole cosmos is believed to be enchanted with spirits and the goal of life is to keep the gods happy. Sacred rituals ensure that the cosmos keeps ticking along in a way that meets your needs. Magical beliefs – that your rituals, thoughts, words, and songs, have a direct impact on the course of the universe, causing the sun to rise and the rains to fall – mark this value system.

This value system is operative during the Prayers of the Community when somebody drops in a request that the Bears win the Super Bowl. It's also apparent in the popular appetite for the DVD *The Secret*, which promises that we can have anything we want simply by "intending" it into existence, which typically translates into fantasies of wheelbarrows full of cash. The positive contribution of this stage is the sensibility that creation is sacred and enchanted.

RED: Warrior Value System (emerged 10,000 years ago)

Out of the collective obedience to the ancestors and the spirits, the need for individual self-expression and the allurement of freedom re-emerges. Think terrible twos. Or in adults, think Rambo and the bevy of films depicting the strong man heroically emerging from the pack. There is no guilt associated with taking exactly what you want. The world is your oyster. Tribal warlords in Iraq, Ethiopia, and Afghanistan, urban street gangs, and prison systems function from this red centre of gravity. Power is exercised as domination. The positive evolutionary contribution of the warrior stage is found in its fierce commitment to individual empowerment and its action orientation.

BLUE: Traditional Value System (emerged 5,000 years ago)

Coming out of the aggression and impulsivity of red, the warrior stage, the life challenge is now for order and purpose. The perceived need is for salvation, law and order. Here the individualist thrust gives way to the needs of the collective. The individual is willing to sacrifice personal pleasure in order to participate in a life of meaning and purpose, delivered by a shared belief in a transcendent cause. The promise that the next life will be better allows us to make sacrifices in this one. The needs of the self are held in balance with the needs of the other. A shift has taken place from the egocentric focus of the warrior (Red) to an ethnocentric outlook – a capacity to take the perspective of the other. But the "other" extends no further than *my* family, *my* tribe, and *my* God. The world is easily polarized into right and wrong, and good and evil.

Seventy percent of the world's religions function out of this value system today. The belief that salvation can happen only through my belief system is a telltale sign of this stage. The contribution of this stage to the spiral is its sense of civic duty, preservation of tradition, respect for authority, loyalty to the group, and deep faith.

ORANGE: Modernist Value System (emerged 300 years ago)

While offering good order and purpose, the collective orientation of the traditionalist value system (Blue) stifled creativity and the innate drive to improve one's lot in life. Adherence to external authority and absolute laws gave way to the so-called modern period.

In the modernist system, rationalists of the Enlightenment distinguished humans from the rest of nature by claiming that we have no inherent limits. Because we can use our God-given reason, our future is not wholly determined by our past experiences or by our station in life. Humanity begins to feel liberated through the discovery that we can shuffle off the chains of a predetermined future to shape one of our own choosing. External authorities, such as the church and her priesthood, lose power. Democracy is born. The rationalists of the Enlightenment declare "no more myths and no more ascent." "No more myths" conveys frustration with the myths and belief systems of the traditionalist (Blue) worldview, which limited human potential. "No more ascent" means that there is no more room for Spirit. The scientific worldview, which believes only in what it can see and touch, replaces the myths of both the warrior (Red) and the traditionalist (Blue) value systems. Humans are declared to be unique in their capacity to shape their own future.

The human being as an *achiever* emerges. We can get what we want through our own strategic thinking and genius. Competition is healthy. The strongest survive. Corporate culture is born. Ambition and ingenuity focused on self paradoxically serves the whole. A rising tide lifts all boats.

The modernist (Orange) value system is the dominant value system in our society today, but you won't find many people functioning out of a purely modernist value system in your congregation because there's no room for Spirit at this level. The positive contribution of this stage is its embrace of reason, its optimism about human potential, and its empowerment of the individual.

GREEN: Postmodernist Value System (emerged 150 years ago, but in full force 40 years ago)

Out of the modernist's (Orange's) fascination with self and the *causa sui* project – to be the cause of oneself – comes a recognition that it can't just be about *me*, and it can't just be about *us*, understood as my family, my country, and my business. It must be about *all of us*, if we're going to survive as a species, and if the earth is going to survive our plundering. The postmodern (Green) value system is world-centric. A shift back to the collective needs of the whole occurs. From the cold rationality of the scientific paradigm, a warmer, kinder self emerges, with the capacity for empathy and sensitivity. Multiple cultures – not just ours – are recognized and validated. Justice, peace, and ecological concerns take precedence in this code. It's the beginning of the postmodern mindset, where everything depends on perspective and context. No single worldview is the correct one – with the exception, we shall see, of the Green worldview. Decision-making is ideally consensual. The problem in the world is understood to be the tendency of the powerful elite to dominate the marginalized. Success and material pleasure take one only so far.

The positive contribution of this stage is its egalitarian and pluralistic sensibility. The congregation and denomination I serve function primarily from a postmodern (Green) centre of gravity.

THE DISQUALIFICATION GAME OF TIER 1

Clare Graves saw these levels (Beige to Green) as belonging to a Tier 1 set of values. They are each, in their own way, focused on their own survival and their own value system as the only legitimate one. The writer of Colossians encourages his followers not to let themselves be "disqualified" by other Christians (Colossians 2:18). These other Christians have accused the Colossians of not eating the right food, observing the correct rituals, or believing the right philosophy (2:8, 16). The writer's response, ironically, is to disqualify the disqualifiers, claiming that it is *their* beliefs that are not Christian (2:8). This is classic Tier 1 thinking.

At the first three levels (survivalist to warrior, or Beige to Red), this disdain for the other levels leads to physical wars and violence. From levels four through to six, (traditionalist to postmodern, or Blue to Green) the result is culture wars.

People at Blue, (the traditionalist stage) criticize those in the stages above them. According to those at Blue, people at Orange (modernists) are "godless" hedonists and people at Green (postmodernists) lack absolute moral values to guide them.

People at Orange (the modern rationalist achievers) find those at Blue to be backward and superstitious, and they judge those at Green (the egalitarian multiculturalists) to be tree-hugging liberal flakes who are good at criticizing but who don't have any real alternatives to economic progress.

Those at the Green level want to deconstruct Orange − after all, look at the harm that corporations and capitalists are doing in the world! They are similarly impatient with the allegiance shown by those at Blue to traditions that serve only to maintain the status quo. Greens believe that they have reached the highest level.

Those at Red, the warriors, just want to blow everybody else up, because the modern/postmodern world has no room for them.

Most "liberal" denominations have a Green centre of gravity. Congregations that are predominantly Green are faced with a dilemma. The tendency of Green to trash all levels below it leaves most liberal congregations criticizing a large number of their own people. Many members operate from an Orange orientation in their business lives, and at a Blue centre in their personal lives (which gets them to church in the first place). These people are typically our highest financial contributors. Out of their Orange ambition and initiative, they often support not only the church, but also the local opera and playhouse, and indeed the very lifestyles we've come to appreciate in the Western world.

I learned from a liberal seminary, which taught from a Green value system, that it was my role to be "prophetic." This meant I essentially took it upon myself to point out all the errors of the warrior, traditionalist, and modernist values systems. (The seminary, of course, didn't use Spiral Dynamics.) This was called "speaking truth to power," following in a long line of Jewish prophets who were called to agitate the ruling elite to remember the poor, the widow, and the orphan. To be sure, this is a noble and sacred calling. But I've seen too many of my colleagues get run out of congregations, and too many supporters of the church just quietly leave, because of what was essentially a values clash.

The importance of Clare Grave's work is that it gives us a language and a set of concepts that allow us, perhaps for the first time, to *consciously* engage our members in a dialogue about value systems instead of unconsciously reacting to our differences. It's one thing for a person such as Ray Anderson, CEO of Interface Incorporated, the largest commercial carpet manufacturing company in the world, to address his corporate colleagues as "fellow plunderers," and to invite them to become more ecological. It's another thing altogether to be bombarded week after week by judgment from the pulpit, to hear again and again the implicit message that you are bad.

Imagine sitting in church, Sunday after Sunday, on the receiving end of criticism because of your *achiever* orientation. It doesn't make any sense to you, because you are a generous person. You may have just given $50,000 to the roof fund of the church. From a modernist value system, you're a hero. From a traditionalist perspective, you're an upstanding citizen, obeying the rules and even willing to give the minister the benefit of the doubt on most issues – he's an authority figure after all. And now you're being bashed from the pulpit. How is this *good* news?

Congregations can also be hard on ministers who have a different value system. Blue-Orange churches chew up and spit out Green ministers on a regular basis. Again, I'm sure this is done without any awareness that a values clash is at the heart of the matter. Until now, we haven't had any language or any way of thinking about this that could help us stop the madness and engage rather in a dialogue about what's happening.

As mentioned, in Tier 1 each value system assumes that the universe reached its zenith when it arrived at them. But these worldviews are the postmodern equivalent of the stations of the cross. We're meant to move through them all in our Christian walk, not get stuck at one. It's an evolving journey, with each station transcending yet including the previous one.

TIER 2 — THE BEING CODES

Clare Grave's research turned up another scale of values that surprised him. In fact, it was so different that he called it Tier 2. In his research, he came across a very small percentage of people (two percent) who made their decision-making at a much more complex level. They thought differently.

YELLOW: Integral Value System (emerged starting 30 years ago)

Out of the communitarian bias of the postmodern values system (Green), a high level individualist thrust emerges in Yellow. Acting out of enlightened self-interest, this individual enjoys the capacity to see the whole spiral. In particular, they recognize that they cannot enjoy a high quality of life when the rest of the spiral is dysfunctional. They see both the dignity and the disaster of each stage, to use philosopher Steve McIntosh's phrase.[3] They see that dysfunctional forms of Red (warrior) and Blue (traditional) lead to fundamentalist revivals and jihads; that Orange (modernist) is messing up the planet with its ambition and technology; and that the Green (postmodern) strategy of trashing the previous levels isn't particularly helpful. But they also see dignity in Red's action orientation, in Blue's sense of moral purpose, and in Green's world-centric vision.

This ability to recognize the validity of each values system and of the spiral as a whole marks the primary difference between Tier 2 thinking and Tier 1 thinking, in which each stage or values system thinks it is the only valid one.

Those with a Yellow (integral) values system are interested in the health of the entire spiral. They appreciate that, from an evolutionary perspective, each level plays an essential role. So why not support the healthiest expression of each? Spiral wizards emerge, such as Don Beck. Beck travels the world teaching strategies that help whole cultures embrace their current values system, and that catalyze growth to the next level. He is currently working in Palestine, with representatives of the Fatah and Hamas movements, teaching them Spiral Dynamics. As well, he and his team significantly influenced the South African leadership, when apartheid was dismantled.

The integral values system (Yellow) is inner-oriented. People at this stage have nothing against authority figures, or moral order, but they are just as likely to listen to a line-worker as the CEO, if they think the line-worker has a great idea. The "flattening" of hierarchies in many businesses reflects this inner-orientation. These people rarely identify with a particular political party. On certain issues they will be conservative; on others they will seem downright socialist. It's very difficult to pigeonhole people with a yellow centre of gravity because they embrace flexibility and flow. Ecopreneurs and social capitalists are a new breed able to integrate the interests of business, people, and the earth. They have an instinctual aversion to all *isms* that freeze the free-flow of ideas and practices. Ethically, they can make judgments that may offend the political correctness of Green, simply because their take on the situation is more nuanced and less concerned with the kind of group-think than can typify Green. They aren't necessarily team players, because the orientation is towards individual creative expression.

Those with a Yellow values system see the potential in an evolutionary philosophy that imbues the universe with a sacred bias toward increased complexity, beauty, and consciousness. They desire to integrate the insights of science and religion, seeing a "pattern that connects" and a deep intelligence that animates the whole universe. They appreciate the difference between dominator hierarchies, such as oppressive regimes and patriarchal value systems, and natural hierarchies

– higher orders emerging spontaneously out of lower orders. Life is therefore about aligning oneself with this evolutionary impulse to transcend and include, and about expressing one's creative gifts.

While there is more dignity to this stage than disaster, it carries the pathological temptation towards elitist thinking and a lack of patience towards those who are "less evolved."

TURQUOISE: Mystical Value System (in the process of emerging)

Yellow still has an individual orientation – let's clean up the spiral in order to enjoy the magnificence of life without worrying about being converted, blown up, or poisoned by pollution. With Turquoise (mysticism), a collective orientation re-emerges. People at this mystical level experience all of life as an expression of a unified whole, of a collective mind seeking expression. Turquoise people get this at a gut and heart level, as well as conceptually. The self is distinct, yes. But it is part of an evolving whole in which everything is connected to all. When physicist Henri Bortoft writes that "the part is the place for the presencing of the whole," a person with a Turquoise orientation immediately understands.

With this stage, humanity has evolved from *me* (Beige through Red), to *us* (Blue and Orange), to *all of us* (late Orange through to late Yellow), to *all that is* (Turquoise/mystical). As with the collective orientation of Blue, there is a willingness to give oneself in service to an organic whole, but the motivation is not for some future reward in the next life. It is to make this one better. Allegiance is not to external authority figures, but to an inner, hidden wholeness. As Jesus affirmed, the kingdom of God is *within*.

The potential disaster of this stage is not actually related to those who have authentically arrived at this stage through spiritual practice and social engagement. It is the temptation of those who have experienced a temporary *state* of mystical awareness to confuse this with a genuine *stage* of development. States are temporary. Stages are permanent as we'll see below.

How could Jesus (or the Buddha or Mohammad or the great Sufi mystics) have operated from a Turquoise level when it is just today in the process of emerging? The problem is that, in an evolutionary universe, enlightenment is a relative phenomenon. One can only be evolved to the highest level of consciousness in existence in any historical period. The solution to this problem requires that we make a distinction between *states* of consciousness – waking, dreaming, deep sleep, and mystical awareness, which are universally available and always have been – and *stages* of consciousness, permanent structures in consciousness that become accessible only after they have been established within a culture and symbolized in cultural artifacts and systems. Repeated profound mystical *state* experiences can lay the foundations for the emergence of a new *stage* of consciousness. I hold out the possibility that there are certain exceptional individuals, such as Jesus, who anticipated and actually began to lay down the foundation for future structures or stages of consciousness that have still not fully emerged.

More typically, enlightenment or awakening is "the realization of oneness with all the states and all the stages that have evolved so far and that are in existence at any given time."[4] Because the universe never stops evolving, more complex stages will emerge out of the mystical stage.

Keep in mind the following points about these value systems.

- Each level or stage contains all the previous levels. We may call upon the positive qualities of any previous system. A person at Yellow (integral) will sometimes want to draw upon the action energy of Red (warrior), the wisdom of good order from Blue (traditional), the ambition and evidence-based data of Orange (modern), and the egalitarian passion of Green (postmodern). At points of stress in our individual lives and in our lives together as congregations, we may also exhibit the dysfunctional qualities of each level – the aggressiveness of the warrior (Red), the rigidity of the traditionalist (Blue), the blind ambition of the modern achiever (Orange), and the political correctness of postmodern (Green). We move up and down the spiral, but have our centre of gravity predominantly at one level.

- These levels describe centres of gravity. When Clare Graves and other developmental psychologists measure levels, if people answer 50 percent of the questions from a particular level, they are considered to be at that level. In other words, someone can be at the Turquoise (mystical) cognitive level, and still have a moral centre of gravity at the Blue (traditionalist) level.

- These are value systems or codes operative in people, and not types of people.

- Most people in postmodern congregations will be averse to accepting these levels, because most are functioning from a Green level, where everybody must be equal and hierarchies are politically incorrect. But this position is untenable, unless one wants to say that Mother Teresa and Osama bin Laden, or George W. Bush and Bishop Desmond Tutu are operating from the same value system. Again, there are dominator hierarchies that must be dismantled, and there are natural hierarchies. This is simply the way the universe evolves.

- You can't skip a stage. There's no leap-frogging when it comes to these levels. Each stage is foundational for the next.

- An emergent dialectic drives the spiral, as the impulse for individual self-expression emerges out of the collective, and then out of the individual orientation, a new, higher-level collective orientation emerges. The warm colours – Red, Orange, and Yellow – are associated with the dynamic of individuation/differentiation. The cool colours – Purple, Blue, Green, Turquoise – are associated with the energy of communion. Each new level transcends but includes the previous levels.

MAPPING IT OUT

1. At Canadian Memorial, the Think Tank generated a list of values with definitions to take to the congregation. All teams, committees, and groups had an opportunity to revise, add, delete. After receiving this input, the Think Tank put the values and definitions on large sheets of Bristol board, one value and definition per sheet. At a congregational weekend retreat, we had participants go around the room, and place stickers on the values that most directly resonated with them, and with their sense of Canadian Memorial. The values with the most stickers made it to our values statement. The one that came up strongly for the congregation that the Think Tank missed was *Fun* – we got the message!

2. Once you have completed your values statement, engage in a conversation about which colour or values system on the spiral dynamics system your values statement represents. This will be your congregation's centre of gravity. Remember that there are also people in the congregation who are at other stages of development. How do you honour them? Talk about the "dignity" and the "disaster" of the stage you are at. How does this manifest in program choices? What sort of programs might you offer, if you chose to intentionally create a climate that would allow the next stage to begin to emerge? Are there any areas of conflict in your congregation that Spiral Dynamics might help to explain?

3. Research indicates that meditation as a spiritual practice is the most effective catalyst to promote movement up the spiral. Is your congregation offering courses on prayer and meditation? Have you considered having an ongoing meditation group?

---

[1] Don Edward Beck and Christopher C. Cowan, *Spiral Dynamics: Master Values, Leadership and Change* (Malden, MA: Blackwell, 1996).

[2] Ibid.

[3] Steve McIntosh, *Integral Consciousness and the Future of Evolution* (St. Paul, Minnesota: Paragon House, 2007), 39.

[4] Ken Wilber, *Integral Spirituality: A Startling New Role for Religion in the Modern and Postmodern World* (Boston: Integral Books, 2007), 179ff.

six

What Colour Is Your Christ?

But who do you say that I am?
~ Matthew 16:15, Jesus of Nazareth ~

Having preached for over 20 years I've often been baffled by people's reactions to my sermons. I'm flattered, of course, when they tell me how much the sermon meant to them. But on occasion an admirer will share what exactly meant so much to them and I can hardly believe what I'm hearing! Not only have they apparently missed the tenor of the sermon, they've heard almost the opposite of what I thought I was saying! What I now realize is that we can only interpret our experience through the lens of the values system that we are operating with at that time in our life. If a preacher delivers a Yellow-oriented sermon (integral) to a Blue-oriented congregation (traditional), they'll make sense of it from within the world of Blue. The Yellow world literally does not exist for the Blue value system.

I had lunch a couple of months ago with a brother in Christ. He is a conservative, open-minded Mennonite who read a book of my sermons and found them very meaningful. But he knew they were coming from a different place. He told me over the course of the lunch that he knew I was a brother in Christ because I used the same words as he did. But a number of the sermons confused him. This man was experiencing cognitive dissonance, an evolutionary pull to integrate at a higher level. (I've experienced this myself with countless teachers.) My greatest fear going into the lunch with him was that he was going to badger me about whether I "knew Christ as my personal Lord and Saviour." But as we shared our appetizer, I sensed a spirit of genuine curiosity – always a sign that a person is open to growth. The truth is that my Christ and his Christ were actually *different*. This is why that question, "Do you know Christ?" is so infuriating. Which Christ?

In what follows, I briefly describe the Christ that people at different stages would "know."

Purple – The Tribal Christ

This Christ is the soul of the world, present in the spirits of animals, plants, the earth, and the sky. He makes the world go 'round when proper ritual is performed. He is the soul of the great ancestors, whose campfires light the starry night sky. Obedience to him is the key to communal life together, the secret of keeping the clan safe from harm, and fed. He answers the prayers of those who are obedient.

Red – The Warrior Christ

Followers of the Red Christ go with him into battle on behalf of their tribe, nation, or belief system. The biblical image of Joshua leading the Hebrews into the Promised Land and fighting other tribes for possession of that land captures the warlord essence of this Christ. The Red Christ led the Christian armies in the crusades. He also led the U.S. army into Iraq. In its most positive expression, following this Christ gives us the energy to "fight" for what we believe in – to take a stand. In its most negative expression, following this Christ has led to the crusades, the Inquisition, the cultural and physical genocide of indigenous people, and current day neo-imperialism.

Blue – The Traditional Christ, a Divine Scapegoat

As part of the divine plan, God sends his only son to suffer and die on behalf of humanity, modelling sacrifice of self for a future reward. The dignity of this Christ is that he brings order and purpose to life for his followers. We learn that there is a plan for life, there is something greater than our own needs and wants to live for. Christ's own sacrifice invites followers to lead lives of self-sacrificial love, with the hope of eternal reward. The "disaster" of this Christ is that he can be used in a triumphalistic manner. He is the *only* truth, the *only* way, and the *only* life, and if you don't believe it you're going to hell.

Orange – The Modern Demythologized Christ and Christ as CEO

There is a dual thrust here. Remember: the Orange values system encompasses both scientific rationalism (no more myths and no more ascent) and the achievist ethic of the industrial revolution. Within this system, Christ is seen as the human one, a teacher of spiritual wisdom. The divinity of Christ is downplayed in favour of the flesh-and-blood human being. In the late 19th and early 20th centuries, there was a strong movement in the church to "demythologize" Christ. Rudolph Bultmann is a representative New Testament scholar of this era. In keeping with the scientific bias of the era, we learned that Christ didn't actually walk on water or actually heal the blind or actually rise from the dead. These are rich metaphors, to be sure, but not to be taken literally. In recent years, the scholars of the Jesus Seminar colour-coded the New Testament writings to determine which belonged to Jesus and which to the early church – an extension of this demythologizing of Christ.

Achievers at the Orange level are interested in Christ not so much for his spirituality, but rather for what they can learn about his leadership style. They are fascinated by Jesus as CEO. He was obviously "successful" in starting a movement, so what was his secret?

In its positive expression, the Orange stage helps us transcend the literalism of the previous levels, grounding our beliefs in something more than wishful thinking. Orange modernist values give us permission to think for ourselves and to realize that we are a centre of creative self-expression. In its negative expression, the Orange level leaves no room for Spirit, for fear of regressing to Blue (traditionalist) and Red (warrior), which it doesn't want to be identified with. It tends, however, to throw the baby (Spirit) out with the bathwater (mythic literalism).

Green – The Egalitarian/Postmodern Christ

The postmodern Christ embraces multiple cultures and downplays the "Truth" of any particular religious system. The Green Christ draws the circle ever wider, so that it includes the outcasts, the left-behinds, and the marginalized. The Green Christ is opposed to most *isms*: sexism, nationalism, racism, elitism, and ageism, to name a few. The only acceptable *isms* are those that are non-hierarchical: egalitarianism, feminism, denominationalism, etc. Postmodernism assumes a global, pluralistic, and multicultural worldview. The Christ of postmodernism has widened his net to include *all of us*, not just *us* (my nation, my tribe, my religion, my family).

In its positive expression, followers of the Green Christ take up the cause of the poor, the left-behinds, and creation. In its negative expression, followers of the Green Christ are impatient and dismissive of all other value systems.

Yellow – The Integral/Ecological/Cosmic Christ

The Yellow, integral Christ encompasses the universe and all cultures as an integrated ecology of systems. This Christ affirms and celebrates the radical interconnectedness of all life. This is the cosmic Christ of Paul's writing, in whom all things are held together. Followers of this Christ become fascinated by the world that the new sciences are discovering, and by how this world connects to the core metaphors and narratives of the Judeo-Christian tradition. They see the integrity of all life, the hidden wholeness that binds us all together – human and other-than-human – in a dance of life. To use another metaphor, Christ is the "pattern that connects." My previous book, *Darwin, Divinity and the Dance of the Cosmos: An Ecological Christianity* was written from the perspective of the ecological/cosmic Christ. The scope of this Christ's concerns and sovereignty is the entire universe. Yet this sovereignty is exercised in a non-coercive, loving manner, so that each creature and every system is free to evolve. The potential downside or "disaster" of this stage is elitist thinking and impatience with those perceived to be "below" this stage.

Turquoise – The Mystical Christ

At this level, the world is experienced – not merely conceptualized – as one. A follower of this Christ does not merely perceive the universe as an integrated whole. She knows herself to be a form of the integrated whole, the part in whom the whole is manifest. The great diversity of life is also an expression of the Holy *One*. All of life is sacred revelation, for those with eyes to see.

The Christ of John's gospel, who expresses a unity between God, the disciples, and himself, reflects this unitive consciousness. (The author of John's gospel clearly enjoyed mystical *states* of consciousness, but interpreted them through a Blue, traditionalist *stage* of development.) This Christ wants his disciples to realize their own Christ-like natures. Worry, which is fear-based, is replaced by joy at the inner awareness that we are manifestations of the Holy *One* playing in the realm of time and space.

The mystical sense "that all shall be well and all manner of thing shall be well" does not issue in a passive stance toward the brokenness of the world. Rather, action that flows from this identification with the Holy Oneness is very effective and efficient. When Paul writes about "letting this mind be in you that was also in Christ," this is the *mind* he was speaking about (Philippians 2:5). Those who are "in Christ" connect naturally with networks of people all over the planet who are living out of this new awareness. Life is full of synchronicities and convergences that no longer surprise. They simply reflect the radical interconnectedness that is God.

The potential disaster of this stage actually resides in those who have enjoyed mystical *states* of consciousness (available at every stage), but who confuse these experiences with a *stage* of consciousness (which are permanent structures in consciousness). We all interpret our experiences through the lens of the stage we are at. Someone at Blue (traditional) may be certain that a mystical experience validates this stage of consciousness as the omega point of development. When this happens, it reinforces the beliefs of this stage as Ultimate Truth, but which are, in fact, only partial truths.

IMPLICATIONS FOR CONGREGATIONAL LIFE

1. After articulating your values statement, your congregation may wish to discern which colour represents your centre of gravity as well as the colour of your Christ. If you're going to try and reach out to those who function from an Orange or modernist values system – perhaps because your church is near a university – then your messaging will be different than if you are trying to reach those who operate from a Green postmodernist system.

2. The reality is that as you move through the stages, the higher the level, the fewer the people you will attract, or have to draw from. Philosopher Ken Wilber estimates that, in the West, 30–40 percent of the population is at Blue (traditional) or lower; 40–50 is at Orange (modern); 20–25 percent is at Green (postmodern), and less than 2 percent is at Tier 2. The more complex the values system, the fewer the people who possess it, and therefore the fewer we have to draw from. This is not an excuse for congregational stagnation or lack of growth. It simply points out that if your centre of gravity is at Yellow (integral), you will need to consider becoming a destination church – a church that people are willing to travel long distances to support and be nurtured by.

3. My hunch is that much of the Orange/modernist population is disillusioned: with materialism (the pursuit of wealth and power), with scientific rationalism (voiding the cosmos of soul and spirit), and with

hyper-individualism (the dog-eat-dog world of neo-Darwinism). But we're not going to speak to them by continually disqualifying them. Show them that the life of the Spirit can be scientific *and* spiritual, that it can honour diversity *and* communion, that there can be moral order *and* individual self-expression, and that material wealth *in the service of spiritual well-being* is their gift to the world.

4. Green does not represent the second coming of Christ. It is one important stage in the developmental arc of ever-more comprehensive values systems and worldviews. Many mainline churches with a Green centre of gravity need to exercise a little more humility, and perhaps allow themselves to evolve.

5. Congregations are uniquely positioned to act as the "conveyer belt," to borrow a phrase from Ken Wilber, that helps to transport individuals from one station (values system) to the next. Wilber uses an intentionally "clunk and grind" metaphor to recognize the fact that this is never a smooth or easy transition. This goal of helping people to move to the next higher stage is consistent with Clare Grave's vision.

> I do suggest…and this I deeply believe is so, that for the overall welfare of total man's existence in this world, over the long run of time, higher levels are better than lower levels and that the prime good of any society's governing figures should be to promote human movement up the levels of human existence."[1]

In other words, we can begin to intentionally function as "attractor" congregations, lighting up people to their next level of spiritual maturity.

PAUL'S GENIUS

Paul, I suspect, would approve. In his famous letter to the Corinthians on the subject of love, he writes, "When I was a child, I spoke like a child, I thought like a child, I reasoned like a child,; when I became an adult, I put an end to childish ways…Now I know only in part; then I will know fully…"

(1 Corinthians 13:11–13). This is implicit evolutionary consciousness. In a similar vein, the author of Hebrews writes about certain people needing to be fed milk, while others are ready for spiritual meat (Hebrews 5:11–14).

Paul has been unfairly criticized by certain groups (representing a Green/postmodern values system primarily) for being regressive in relation to slaves, women, and the relationship of the church to the state. For one thing, it is crucial to distinguish between the genuine letters (which Paul definitely wrote); the conservative letters (of disputed authorship); and the reactionary letters, where women are told to be silent and slaves are instructed to obey their masters (which were definitely not written by Paul). But even in Romans, an authentic Pauline letter, Paul displays a more conservative approach in relation to paying taxes to the state. In Chapter 13, for example, he instructs the community to be "subject to the governing authorities" and to "pay taxes, for the authorities are God's servants" (Romans 13:1, 6). It is reasonable to assume that the severe consequences of implementing the gospel ideal of equality in a patriarchal Roman culture caused Paul to moderate the radical egalitarianism of Christ. Without compromising the radicality of the ideal, Paul picked his battles. The subversive ideal still waits to be fully implemented in our day and age.

It can be argued that Paul took a sophisticated and realistic approach to the issues and institutions he faced. Yes, to be in Christ is to transform social structures and systems in the direction of greater equality. On the evolutionary path to equality, Paul acted as a conveyer belt. Even as he himself realized the radical nature of what it meant to be in Christ, on the way to full equality, he helped men to treat women with greater respect and dignity, slave-owners to treat their slaves as brothers and sisters in Christ, and the church to respect but not worship the state. He displayed great patience and wisdom in ushering his people forward.

Furthermore, he handled the Gentile problem brilliantly, convincing the leaders in Jerusalem that non-Jews could receive and embody the gospel of Jesus Christ. Because of Paul, Peter had his powerful dream in which he heard from God that he was to declare no animal unclean that God had made clean. Paul transcended the ethnocentric stage of development (Red/Blue) and anticipated the world-centric stage of Green. It is difficult for us to appreciate just how radical this shift around dietary laws was for a first-century Jew. All of these "baby steps" were essential in moving the early church to embody a more inclusive and compassionate Christ.

The problem lies not with Paul. Rather, subsequent generations of imperial Christians chose not to continue Paul's evolutionary and revolutionary process of intentionally shepherding believers to the next stage of their evolutionary journey.

Today, 75 percent of the Christian church worldwide is frozen at a mythic/literal stage of development. Ken Wilber's understanding of why we're stuck at such a low level of spiritual intelligence in the West is compelling.[2] Basically, he argues that because universities have historically operated from the scientific rational level of Orange, there has been no room for Spirit. Academics exist to refute Red (warrior) and Blue (traditional) spirituality. Consequently, even though they are Orange, their own spiritual intelligence gets frozen at the lower mythic level, because they imagine that these levels exhaust the life of the Spirit.

Young people go to these institutions of higher learning with spiritual yearnings, but are forced to choose between the spiritual wasteland of Orange academia and the mythic literalism of Red and Blue. In either case, we end up with leaders of the developed world who have either rejected what they associate with Christianity – Red and Blue – or are leading the world with very limited spiritual intelligence. One doesn't have to look any further than the Bush administration for proof. And to be honest, it's no different in the Canadian context.

The point of articulating our values system and of using Grave's model is not to be elitist. The egoic concern of elitism is a Tier 1 concern, in fact. Rather, I search the world for those who dwell within a values system and related worldview that is more comprehensive, nuanced, and sophisticated than mine. I will do this for the rest of my life. The truth is that, in an evolutionary paradigm, we never arrive. New, more comprehensive levels will always emerge out of existing levels in order to deal with the new challenges and stresses that arise. This is emergence in action. The problems will never disappear. They will get more complex in fact. Furthermore, the Christ who is cosmic in scope and the presence of universal wisdom will always serve the image we have constructed for him. Therefore, we must never freeze the image of Christ into one timeless form. With Christ, there is no place to rest our head and no value system that will not be transcended by a more comprehensive one.

Hafiz, a 14th-century Sufi mystic, wrote a poem from a mystical state of consciousness, but with a warning at the end about the perils of elitist thinking.

Why Aren't We Screaming Drunks?[3]

*The sun once glimpsed God's true nature
And has never been the same.*

*Thus the radiant sphere
Constantly pours its energy
Upon this earth
As does He from behind
The veil.*

*With a wonderful God like that
Why isn't everyone a screaming drunk?*

Hafiz's guess is this:

*Any thought that you are better or less
Than another man*

*Quickly
Breaks the wine
Glass.*

MAPPING IT OUT

1. Using the colour-coding, how would you answer Christ's question: "Who do you say that I am?" for yourself?

2. Which Christ describes your congregation's centre of gravity?

3. In what ways are you acting as an "attractor" congregation, meeting newcomers where they are at, but helping them to evolve in the direction of a more comprehensive Christ?

4. How does your congregation act as a "conveyor belt" helping followers of Christ to evolve?

5. Do an audit of your congregation's style and the content of your worship services through the lens of the question, "What colour is your Christ?" Include prayers, preaching, hymns, time with the children, Communion liturgy, the greeting and commissioning.

6. Meet in groups of two or three, with each group representing a different colour – from Blue (traditional) to Yellow (mystical). Prepare yourselves to make "an account of your faith" to the other groups. Describe the Christ you follow: what is of ultimate importance, what is good, what is true, and what is beautiful from your perspective in life? What kind of spiritual practices would you like to see in your congregation from the perspective of your Christ? Report back, listening non-judgmentally to each other.

---

[1] Don Edward Beck and Christopher C. Cowan, *Spiral Dynamics: Master Values, Leadership and Change*, (Malden, MA: Blackwell, 1996), 35.

[2] Ken Wilber, *Integral Spirituality: A Startling New Role for Religion in the Modern and Postmodern World* (Boston: Integral Books, 2007), 186ff.

[3] Hafiz, *The Gift: Poems by Hafiz*, Daniel Ladinsky, trans. (New York: Penguin Press, 1999), 205.

seven

The Angel of Your Congregation: Morphic Fields in Communities of Faith

The seven stars are the angels of the seven churches.
~ Revelation 1:20 ~

*Therefore, since we are surrounded by so great
a cloud of witnesses...
let us run with perseverance the race that is set before us.*
~ Hebrews 12:1 ~

I walked into our Centre for Peace a few weeks ago and found a woman sitting in a chair blissfully looking around. I approached her and asked if I could be of assistance. She told me that she was very intuitive and that the "vibration" within the building was so pleasing to her that she had decided to just sit for a while and enjoy it. (Remember, we're in Vancouver – the left coast!) She said the energy felt like a balance of Shiva and Shakti energy – the divine masculine and feminine in Hinduism.

For those of us who work at the Centre, encounters like I had with this woman are no longer surprising. The building is filled day and night with sacred chanting circles; Tai Chi, meditation, and yoga groups; corporate visioning retreats by companies wanting to go green; personal growth workshops; and luminaries from various spiritual disciplines sharing their wisdom. Many people comment on the peaceful "vibe" in the building.

These various groups establish an energy field that is palpable to those who are sensitive to such things. You actually *do* get a *vibe* from organizations. People walk through the church door for the first time and talk about "feeling at home." Some start to weep. Others feel like their creative energies are sparked. What's going on?

In the old scientific worldview of Sir Isaac Newton, space was empty. It was no more than the inert distance between two objects. The objects were real, but space was just dead space.

Science has since discovered this understanding couldn't be more wrong. Space is composed of four fundamental fields that literally give shape and form to the universe – the strong and weak nuclear fields, the gravitational field, and the electromagnetic field. We live and move and have our being within these extremely powerful yet invisible fields, which connect everything and everybody. Furthermore, quantum physics has discovered that these fields of connectedness are anything but inert. They are fecund. We have our being in a cosmic vacuum that is neither empty, nor inert. It is a generative matrix, from which life pops into and out of existence. We exist in living fields.

Dr. Rupert Sheldrake, a biologist who also happens to be Christian, has been doing research for 20 years on what he calls "morphic fields." His work in this area began as he was studying what biologists call morphogenesis, the coming into being of form. He asked himself, "How do plants grow from simple embryos into the characteristic form of their species? How do their flowers develop in such different ways?" Neo-

Darwinist biology posits that it's all in the genes. Sheldrake didn't think this was sufficient to account for the differences in how they developed. He posited that invisible morphic fields retained the memory of a species, like an invisible blueprint that underlies the form of a living system.

This is the new scientific version of the function of soul in the philosophy of Aristotle and the theology of St. Thomas Aquinas. The soul of the oak tree was believed to draw the tree toward its mature form. The soul was the organizing principle for every life form. Sheldrake's research has led him to theorize that every organism, individual, and organization taps into the field of its predecessors, and contributes to the evolution of the morphic field through its own self-expression. In other words, when I came to Canadian Memorial 12 years ago, I entered into its morphic field, an invisible yet powerful field of memories, behaviours, and activities that in-formed the current configuration of the congregation. The morphic field – generated by the articulation and enactment of the mission, vision, and values – is the organizing principle of a congregation. It is further shaped by the dynamic, historical relationship between past generations of believers and the colour of the existing congregation's Christ. To use St. Thomas Aquinas' analogy, the present vision and mission in combination with the historic "field" created by earlier generations, act as a kind of congregational soul drawing the community toward ever fuller expressions on its evolutionary path.

Through a process Sheldrake calls "morphic resonance," these fields of the past and present intersect, interact, and influence one another. In other words, the fields themselves evolve, or at least have the capacity to do so. When you intentionally update your mission, vision, and values statements in the kind of process I have described in previous chapters, you are consciously evolving the morphic field of your congregation.

On a practical level, this means that when new members join your congregation they "download" the field. You don't actually need to teach them the vision, mission, and values didactically (although this is not a bad idea). They will intuitively "get" what the congregation is about.

The more individuals within a congregation align themselves with the mission, vision, and values, and see themselves as ambassadors of this vision, the stronger the morphic field becomes. If the congregation's centre of gravity is Green, Yellow, or Turquoise, that is colour of the Christ that newcomers will tap into. The morphic field will also determine the kind of people you attract to your congregation. When the field becomes strong enough, people will feel the transformative power of the living Christ, inviting them to lives of compassion and service.

A well-known, if apocryphal, story is told about monkeys in Borneo learning to use their thumbs. At the very same time, on the other side of the planet, other monkeys started using *their* thumbs. According to morphic field theory, these other monkeys had tapped into the "monkey field," which had been updated by the Borneo monkeys. Similarly, every time a person enters your sanctuary for worship or prayer they tap into the field of your congregation. Again, Sheldrake is doing compelling research which supports that subjective intuition that these fields are real and powerful. I would say that the primary purpose of the church board, in fact, is to help strengthen and evolve this field through their spiritual practice, policy-making, and Christian witness.

THE ANGEL OF YOUR CONGREGATION

Walter Wink, a theologian, has written about how each congregation has an angel.[1] He noticed that in the book of Revelation the author writes not to the congregations, but to the *angel* of each congregation (Revelation 2:1, 8, 12, 18; 3:1, 7, 14). Wink suggests that the angel is the corporate personality of the congregation. An angel may be parsimonious or generous, cranky or compassionate, serious or playful, rebellious or conventional. The point he's making is that the author of Revelation knew that there was no use trying to make changes in these congregations without going through the angel. The angel of the congregation may be in need of *metanoia* every bit as much as any individual within the congregation. In other words, you have to shift the culture or morphic field before transformation is possible.

Rupert Sheldrake plays with this idea in a book he co-authored with Matthew Fox called *The Physics of Angels*.[2] Sheldrake speculates that each morphic field, at the biological and cultural level, has an overseeing angel associated with it, which exists to connect the individual form with the field, and to form a bridge between the field and the Holy Spirit.

Here's another thing to remember about morphic fields. Sheldrake reminds us that they are essentially the *habits* of an individual, organism, or an organization – habits that are intended to evolve, yes, but habits nonetheless. Don't confuse them with the Holy Spirit. If the "angel" of the field and the field itself get stuck, the individual members will also get stuck or frozen at a particular stage of development. When your mission, vision, and values process is animated by the Spirit, you will inevitably come up against the habits of the morphic field that resist evolution.

It helps to keep these habits of the morphic field in mind when you are in the throes of culture shifting and you run up against individuals who are digging in their heels. These people are manifesting the old field, acting as mouthpieces for intransigent angels in need of conversion. Don't take it personally. They are signalling to you where the resistance is in the field. Figure out ways to speak through them to the angel that has sent them. Become curious, not defensive. Listen to their specific concerns – you may be entertaining angels unaware!

MAPPING IT OUT

1. What words would you use to describe the angel of your congregation?

2. What's the "vibe" that your congregation gives off?

3. What "colour" is your angel?

4. Have a dialogue with your angel. Use the Gestalt technique of putting your angel in an empty chair across from you and speak to it. Then trade places. Sit in the empty chair and respond as the angel. Let yourself go! You're playing with Spirit.

5. What are the bad habits of your angel?

6. How is your angel in need of conversion?

[1] Walter Wink, *The Powers That Be: Theology for a New Millennium* (New York, Doubleday, 1998), 3.

[2] Rupert Sheldrake and Matthew Fox, *The Physics of Angels: Exploring the Realm Where Science and Physics Meet* (New York: HarperCollins Publishers, 1996), 20.

eight

Setting Our Face toward Jerusalem:
The Psychological Foundations
of Leadership

Jesus set his face toward Jerusalem.
~ LUKE 9:51 ~

Not long after arriving in Vancouver, British Columbia, from Toronto, Ontario, I had a dream. In the dream, a young couple (who were at the time members of Canadian Memorial) approach me with the news that I have been selected to go to Ottawa, Ontario, the capital of Canada. I tell them that it is a ridiculous idea. I have just arrived in Vancouver and have no intention of moving to Ottawa. They tell me that I don't understand. When you're selected to go to Ottawa, you go to Ottawa. I protest and I cry, but inside I know that I really have no choice.

When I worked with my dream, my biggest fear was that I had made a poor choice in coming to this new congregation. But then I realized that I was taking the dream too literally. The young couple in the dream was very politically engaged. When I thought metaphorically about the city of Ottawa, I realized that it is the seat of power in our country; it's where our parliament and senate sit. The literal interpretation wasn't nearly as frightening as this metaphorical one. In being called "to Ottawa" I was being invited to find my own seat of power. Travelling 3,000 miles geographically would have been easy compared to the psychological and spiritual journey I was being asked to take. I needed to change my leadership style if this congregation was going to undergo a culture shift and become an emerging congregation. Jesus' most difficult journey was to Jerusalem. Mine would be to "Ottawa."

Previous to this, I hadn't consciously considered what it meant to be a leader. In seminary, I learned not a single thing about leadership. (It is remarkable to me that our seminaries have just started to teach about leadership in the last couple of years. Talk about throwing sheep to the wolves!) I was ill-prepared to be a leader when I was ordained and placed in my first congregation. My job, I thought, was to preach, visit as many people as humanly possible, teach the odd course, and make sure good order was maintained in the congregation. I was prepared to discuss theology – a skill I discovered that held moderate interest for most congregational members. My head was ready, but my heart and my gut would have to learn about leadership the hard way.

I've sometimes experienced an unconscious bias against leadership in my denomination. This goes back to the worldview of the Green value system. If there are leaders, then we're not all equal. Leadership, therefore, is by definition hierarchical, and everybody knows that this is a bad thing.

But leadership is one of the many gifts the Spirit gives to the Body of Christ – along with apostleship, service, teaching, proclaiming the word, prophecy, and others (1 Corinthians 12:4–11). On the other hand, just because it's a gift doesn't mean that we cannot be intentional about cultivating it.

The mainline church is suffering from a crisis of leadership. This is not to say that we don't have many wonderful people, both lay and clergy, who are leading congregations. We do. But we need more leaders who are ready, willing, and able to take a stand and stick with it. We need leaders who can withstand the wrath of the most critical members of their congregations, or of the ones who threaten to withhold their financial offering, and discover that it was not much more than a tempest in a teapot. Jesus asked his followers what they expected when they saw John the Baptist: "A reed shaken by the wind?... A prophet? Yes, I tell you, and more than a prophet. This is the one about whom it is written, 'See, I am sending my messenger ahead of you, who will prepare your way before you'" (Luke 7:24–27).

We need John's chutzpah for the 21st century. The congregational leader's job is to go out into the storm, and not be blown about by the winds of opinion, criticism, and opposition. We are preparing the way for Christ to enter the hearts and minds of our people. John didn't win any popularity contests (and we may not either!). He called the religious leaders of his day a "brood of vipers" – to their faces! He told Herod that his current living arrangement was flat out wrong, for which he was decapitated.

Most attempts at culture-shifting crash and burn because there inevitably comes a point when a tough decision must be made and nobody is willing to make it. In fact, there are usually a series of tough decisions to make – and after the decisions are made, the capacity to hold to them in the face of multiple efforts to sabotage them is required. Leadership is not a popularity contest and moments like this test our resolve.

I don't mean to suggest by this that in order to make these decisions, or to keep to them, we have to be hard-nosed or antagonistic, or that we have to dominate others through the strength of our will. This is not leadership; it is tyranny. But I can't begin to count the stories I've heard from colleagues about how "they tried, but it didn't work" in the congregations they were leading. When I listen carefully to what didn't work, nine times out of ten I can to trace the problem back to a failure to make a tough call, and/or a failure to stick with a decision in the face of opposition.

In 1988, our denomination decided to ordain gay and lesbian persons. At the time, I was in my first congregation, a once-tiny rural church around which the city had developed. I knew that I had to preach about the decision, and decided that I would invite feedback right after the sermon. That sermon was not easy to preach it, nor was it easy to face the feedback. The very first person to stand up after I finished was a pillar of the congregation and one of its stronger financial supporters. He said that it was one of the finest sermons he had ever heard: well-crafted, delivered with passion, and the congregation was fortunate to have me as their minister. Then came the hammer: "Oh, and one last thing – this is the last sermon I will ever listen to in this congregation!" He turned and walked out of the service. He wasn't the only one who left as a consequence of that sermon. It was painful, but I believe I made the right decision. And, it was just a taste of what was to come in future congregations.

The decision to ordain gay and lesbian clergy was made by the national court of my denomination. So while it was painful to discover that the personal charms and rhetorical skills I possessed were not enough to please everybody, I didn't have to take responsibility for the decision.

Many of us struggled a decade or so ago with introducing inclusive language. A colleague tells the story of when he tried to experiment with the Lord's Prayer. He introduced alternative translations from the original Aramaic, slowly helping people to understand that the Holy Spirit didn't write the King James Version. He still remembers the first Sunday he printed a version of the prayer with the opening line rendered as, "*Our Loving God, in whom is heaven.*" You'd think he had taken all the Bibles out of the pews and burned them in the parking lot. From certain quarters the opposition was intense. Some people even threatened to go down the road to the Presbyterians, who would never dream of changing the Lord's Prayer! But here's a lesson I've learned the hard way: for every person who has ever left a congregation because of a decision they didn't like, two more have joined because of that same decision.

I don't want to give the impression that sticking by a tough decision is easy, least of all for me. In fact, being a "pleaser" is my psychological default position. That's why the dream about going to Ottawa was so threatening for me. Prior to the dream, I tended to capitulate to the needs and wants of others, to the point of being unaware of my own needs and wants. This new way of being was stretch, believe me. Going to Ottawa, so to speak, caused me great grief. In the second congregation I served, I seriously contemplated leaving the ministry, because being authentic to who I felt God was calling me to be was definitely not pleasing many members of the congregation. I didn't think I could survive the onslaught of disapproval. Here's a song I wrote that expresses how difficult it was for me to go to Ottawa, to stop being a pleaser.

Burnout

Refrain
It's one more cup of coffee, two more Tylenol,
a rum and coke and *Chicago Hope*,
that'll help me to forget it all.
I'm just a low-grade junkie, underneath this preacher's gown;
I ain't nobody special and there ain't no good news goin' down, so…
Please, take this robe; it's too heavy for me;
and please, take this stole, I long to be free.

1. Now Rev. Tom, he sure could preach; told it the way it was,
and Bill before him, what a gem! you don't find many men like *them*.
We like the old hymns thanks a lot, cause God's a He, (a She He's not!).
And we'll take our preacher's straight, not gay; St. Paul says that's the only way.

2. It's too much for my ego; my skin's a little thin,
I'm tired of being target practice for Pollyannas and redneck men.
I don't remember choosing this life; I'd rather be laying sod,
than standing up here Sunday morning, preaching on behalf of God, so…

Refrain

3. Please come for a visit, our committee sure needs you
My Uncle Tom's in the hospital and Mrs. Avery is feeling blue,
Charlie's feeling left out, he's our Randall Hurst;
So get it straight who's got the pull; in this place the first shall be first.

4. I'm fresh out of ideas, I just ran out of care,
that ain't the truth you're looking for, but maybe there ain't no truth
out there.
I'm sorry, Mama; I tried to please you, Dad;
The Golden Boy is falling fast,
I'm one part wheat and three parts chaff.

Refrain
It's one more cup of coffee, two more Tylenol,
a rum and coke and *Chicago Hope*,
that'll help me to forget it all.
I'm just a low-grade junkie, underneath this preacher's gown;
I ain't nobody special and there ain't no good news goin' down, so...
Please, take this robe; it's too heavy for me;
and please, take this stole, I long to be free.

The most important training for ministry did not occur for me at
seminary. Seminary prepared me to think theologically, for which I am
grateful. But it didn't prepare me to stand in the winds of opposition
and not be shaken. It didn't prepare me to deal with the reality that
some people would flat out dislike me. It didn't prepare me for the truth
that when you put on a gown and a stole, people start projecting their
mothers and their fathers, and their abusive grandfathers on to you.
It didn't prepare me for women who interpret my attention as sexual
interest. It didn't prepare me to set limits on what I will and will not do,
or teach me how to stay connected with people who scream at me. It

didn't help me to articulate my own values, where I stood on important issues, so I could calmly state those when the chair of the Board told me I was just plain wrong. It didn't prepare me to confront a staff person when that person was not able to live out of the congregation's vision.

What *did* prepare me for leadership was a training program for pastoral counselling, which, at the time, was offered by the Canadian Association for Pastoral Education (CAPE), now the Canadian Association for Pastoral Practice and Education (CAPPE). As part of this program, I learned stage theories of human development. I was required to articulate my feelings as well as my thoughts. I sat in an interpersonal relations group and processed the inevitable conflicts that arose in that group, along with all the other feelings that emerge when human beings do life deeply together. I learned how to listen deeply. I learned when I was projecting my own stuff onto others.

At the same time, I did three intensive years of personal therapy to help me sort out my issues arising from my family of origin. I discovered why I had such a need to please others, and why I couldn't ask for what I needed. I recovered my passion for life and learned the trigger points that cause me to regress into dysfunctional patterns. I figured out why I get depressed, and that it doesn't take a major event to trigger the depression. I learned to express my anger. The most difficult learning of all was around opening my heart and all that stands in the way of keeping it open.

Some people might say that this is psychological work, not spiritual work. Some think that spiritual direction or companionship is the answer. And it is – for some. But too often this "spirituality" is built upon a shaky psychological foundation. Under pressure it turns into sentimentality, preciousness, being "nice," and soft-pedalling real differences. One's relationship with God might be tight, but this doesn't necessarily translate into effective leadership.

We evolve along different lines of human development – moral, psychological, spiritual, aesthetic, cognitive, and physical, to name a few. In my experience, seminary mainly addresses the cognitive line and leaves it up to the seminarian to work on the others. Yet we skip over doing our psychological work at our peril and, more importantly, at the peril of the congregations we serve.

There is simply no getting around it. A congregation can only develop to the depth of the capacity of its leadership, lay or clergy. Occasionally, I see a congregation that develops despite its minister, but when this is happening there is strong lay leadership present. Leaders need to develop along all the lines mentioned above, but without strong skills in the psychological/relational line, their work will be compromised.

LEADING FROM WITHIN AND THE CORE CAPACITIES
OF LEADERSHIP

There is no such thing as a handbook that will give us all the techniques we need to lead a congregation. Which is fine, because leadership is not about *technique*. It's about *personhood*. Leadership comes from *within*. What's more, there are no shortcuts we can take on the road to becoming fully human. It's tough work and it takes a lifetime.

Otto Scharmer has written a book on deep organizational change that is destined to become a classic. The book is called *Theory U*.[1] As a way to discuss and learn about leadership, Scharmer uses the image of a painter standing before a painting. We can look at the *results*, the painting itself, and try to duplicate it. We can analyze the *method*, the process the artist employed to paint the picture, and try to teach it. Or – and this has been the "blind spot" of leadership research – we can focus on what's going on *within* the artist as he stands before a blank canvas. Until now, we have virtually ignored what's going on *within* the artist/leader. This is primarily because most researchers operate out of the Orange modernist level, and Orange is blind to spirit. But this is precisely the point at which we enter into profound spiritual mystery – the generative source out of which all creativity and all leadership emerges.

As part of his research, Scharmer spoke with the late CEO of Hanover Insurance, Bill O'Brien. "Bill helped me understand that what counts is not only *what* the leaders do and *how* they do it, but their *interior condition*, the inner source from which they operate or the *source* from which all of their actions operate."[2] Cultivating our "interior condition" requires at least four psychological core capacities:

1. self-definition
2. staying connected across differences or differentiation
3. emotional intelligence, and
4. awareness of our "shadow."

I am indebted to the work of my colleague and friend Rev. Anna S. Christie for her brilliant synthesis of the work of Murray Bowen (family systems theory), Leslie Greenberg (attachment theory and emotionally focused therapy), and emotional intelligence (Daniel Goleman). For a more in-depth discussion of leadership, I recommend her book *Evoking Change*.[3]

Self-Definition

Self-definition is the capacity to say I am this and not that. I believe this, but I don't believe that. I want this and am not interested in that. I can do this, but I can't do that. All sorts of things get in the way of this kind of clarity of personhood. For example, I find in myself a tendency to assume that other people cannot handle my power. In my worst moments, I believe that if I am crystal clear about myself, then it will cause others to lose their own identity. As a result, I am tempted to moderate my self-definition, my position, my belief, or my stand, so as not to overwhelm the other person. This, of course, is crazy – and crazy-making for myself and for the other person. When this kind of behaviour becomes habitual, and it can, we gradually lose any sense of our own centre. I am not responsible for anybody else's self-definition, and it is arrogant to assume that my strong sense of self diminishes another person.

Most of us know when we are in the presence of somebody who has fallen out of the practice of defining themselves clearly. There is a palpable *absence of presence*. We experience the other person as a mush-ball with no edges, no "point" of view, and no centre. This kind of person saps our energy as we try desperately to determine if anybody is home.

Staying Connected

The capacity for self-definition is closely associated with differentiation or the ability to stay connected across differences. It's one thing to define oneself clearly. It's another thing to stay connected to those whose self-definition is different than mine. When I preach, I take positions on issues. People pretty much know where I stand. Many will disagree. For example, I took a position on both of the U.S. invasions of Iraq and stated my opposition openly from the start. Some people walked out. Others told me that I shouldn't be taking political stands from the pulpit. Our largest financial donor told me over lunch that he didn't approve.

Avoiding those who disagree with us is one of the worst things we can do. The most difficult lesson I've learned in 20 years of ministry is to pick up the phone, hop in the car, or ride my bike to meet with someone who is angry with me. (Do not e-mail!) Acknowledge the disagreement: "I understand that you're not happy with something I said, or with how the vote went. When would you like to talk about it?" It's easy to bury one's head in the sand and hope that the conflict will blow over – it *never* does – or to take a stand and then adopt a "screw you" attitude toward those who disagree. It's much harder to take a stand and to listen to a beloved member of the congregation express disappointment or anger with you. But if there is one secret to congregational stability, this is it.

Emotional Intelligence

Emotional intelligence refers to the capacity to know what you are feeling, to be able to appropriately express these feelings, and to be able to take responsibility for your feelings. It's rare that a congregation will melt down over an issue. But it will melt down depending on how the feelings around the issue are managed.

A surprising number of people in leadership positions are unaware of their feelings. My wife and I lead pre-marriage workshops. One of the things we've discovered is that men have a tendency to reduce all feelings to anger, while women have a tendency to reduce all feelings to sadness (although women, by and large, enjoy more access to wider range of feelings). I notice that when someone cuts Ann off in traffic, she expresses fear. When the same happens to me, I express anger, although truthfully my deepest feeling is fear. Also, when women are asked how they feel about their fiancé or husband watching four hours of sports on a Sunday afternoon, they will typically say they feel sad or disappointed. It takes a lot of work to help them get in touch with their anger.

A feeling is just that, an actual physical sensation that manifests in bodily signals – tears for sadness, clenched muscles for anger, a bowed head for shame, a red face for embarrassment, an open heart for joy. In the process of socialization, both within families and in institutions, we are sent messages about which feelings are safe to feel and which are not. Part of the work of leadership is learning that *all* feelings are okay. They are physical signals that give us crucial information about our experience. If we are unable to receive that information, we will find ourselves behaving incongruently – we will be "out of touch."

One of the differences between animals, toddlers, and adult humans is that the latter have the capacity to receive information about feelings, and to make choices about what to do with them. As adults, we are freed from the tyranny of the limbic system, the mammalian part of our brain that knows essentially only two ways to respond to threat: fight or flight. We have a gland in this part of the brain called the amygdala, which means "almond," referring to its size and shape. The amygdala evolved for one primary purpose: to protect us from danger. Once this little guy gets triggered, it takes only 1/5000 of a second to start the physiological ball rolling. Adrenalin is released and blood flows away from our heart and brain to our limbs to prepare us to fight or run. When it's triggered, we literally get stupid, because of this flow of oxygen away from our brain.

The trick is to get the neocortex – the distinctively human part of our brain responsible for reason and logic – firing. The problem is that the amygdala outguns the neocortex when we perceive that we are in danger. Before the neocortex has a chance to engage in reason, this little almond gland hijacks us. Now, this is handy when a Tyrannosaurus Rex has us lined up for his next meal. Unfortunately, the amygdala doesn't differentiate between an actual monster and our mother-in-law. And yes, there is a difference! It's why a 50-year-old man can get apoplectic over a phone call from his mother. He's in no physical danger, but the amygdala makes virtually no distinction between emotional and physical danger. In 1/5000 of a second, before he's consciously aware of what he's doing, he's defending his life for all its worth, and in the process, saying things he will regret later. He hurts his poor mom simply because he couldn't manage his amygdala. Emotional intelligence means taking responsibility for our evolutionary equipment.

We can engage the evolutionary gift of the neocortex and make rational choices. If we are emotionally mature, these choices will be *congruent* with the feelings, but not *determined* by them. Developing emotional literacy means that we *feel* our feelings, but we can also talk *about* them. This ability to objectify our feelings – to get some distance from them and to deal with them as information – is a distinctive capacity of adult humans. Whereas babies and toddlers *are* their impulses, adult *have* impulses.

This means, among other things, that nobody outside of me is responsible for my feelings. Another person can't *cause* my anger. My anger is *my* emotional response to something someone has done or said. Another person in the room, hearing or experiencing exactly the same thing, might have a totally different response from me, or a totally neutral response. When I first starting dating my present wife, Ann, she had two teenage children. One evening, after a movie and dinner, we returned to her home to find her daughter, Mary, sitting in front of the fire, reading a book. It looked cozy and warm. So I sat down beside her to make conversation. Mary turned to Ann and said, "Mom, I negotiated to have this time alone this evening. You and Bruce are not welcome." I was devastated. Ann was unphased. Mary did not cause my feelings of rejection, shame, and anger. They were *my* feelings, which reflected issues related to my own family of origin.

The Shadow

Finally, we all carry around within us what Swiss psychologist Carl Jung called "the shadow archetype." These are all the disowned feelings, experiences, impulses, and desires that accumulate in our psyches in the process of socialization.

None of us make it to adulthood unscathed. We were pretty much left to our own devices to negotiate our way into adulthood the best we could. In the process, we internalized from our various environments a sense of what is good and bad, right and wrong, pure and impure, sacred and profane. When our own impulses, desires, behaviours, and experiences conflicted with these messages, we had no choice but to lock them up in the basement of our psyches. There, in the subterranean darkness, our shadow took shape – hidden, but powerfully operative, precisely because it calls the shots from the basement, outside of our conscious awareness.

For example, when ministers, or any congregational member, have unconscious, negative associations with their sexual energy, they disown their sexuality. Disowned sexuality inevitably begins to "leak" out in the form of furtive glances, innocent flirting, a hand that lingers on a shoulder a little too long. When confronted, the person will protest that this is preposterous. Sexual interest was the furthest thing from his or her mind. And it's actually true. It was the furthest thing from his or her *conscious* mind. Shadow work involves surfacing these disowned feelings and dealing with them consciously.

Again, many ministers bring with them assumptions about what is "holy" and about how they should *be* as a minister. Power is bad.

Ambition is bad. Greed is bad. But what does the minister do with the fact that as a human being she is allured by power and ambition and wealth? She likes things to go her way. She secretly wants that position at national office.

A lot of sermons get preached by the shadow. Typically, they are full of judgment, condemnation, and holier-than-thou attitudes. The quickest way to identify your shadow is to notice what makes you angry, what elicits your moral judgment, what it is that you simply cannot tolerate in others. These things are often a sign of what you can't accept about yourself – your dissociated shadow.

Jesus and the Shadow

Jesus was doing shadow work when he went out into the wilderness to be tempted by "Satan" (Luke 4:1–11). Psychologically, Satan can be understood as the shadow in one's own psyche. The story says that Satan was testing Jesus, but in truth, Jesus was testing himself, to see if he was ready for public ministry.

What was Jesus' shadow? It focused around security; trust in God; and power, status, and wealth. How do we know this? Because these are precisely the things that Satan threw in Jesus' face in the wilderness. Jesus had to face these things directly, that is *consciously*. If he didn't go through this experience, then when faced with his own physical hunger, he would be tempted to set up a kiosk in his hometown and use his special powers as a tourist attraction to generate steady pay and three meals a day (Luke 4:3–4). (This was a common practice among those considered to have magical powers.) If he hadn't faced his own desire for power, then this disowned desire would have clouded his focus on *God's* kingdom (4:8–11). If he hadn't faced his lack of trust in God, then he would have been constantly testing God in his ministry (4:5–7).

Jesus lacking trust? Desiring the kingdoms of the world? Tempted by security issues? Yep. Just like you and me. Shadow work is tough work, but if Jesus had to go through it, is there any reason why we should be spared?

INTO THE FIRE

Our core capacities – our ability to self-define, stay connected, exhibit emotional intelligence, and deal with our shadow – will be sorely tested as we go about developing an emergent culture in our congregations.

Shortly after I arrived at Canadian Memorial, a team of 12 people developed a music vision. We wanted a minister of music with spiritual presence, one who was interested in and capable of providing a wide range of musical styles, from classical to gospel, jazz, pop, and sacred chant. To make a long, complicated, and painful story short, we decided to serve notice to the beloved director of music who had served the congregation for over 20 years. Five choir members and a few congregational members left and never returned.

The story gets even more painful. The fellow we hired to replace the former director of music was a virtuoso organist, but contrary to what we heard in the interview, he showed very little interest in any styles of music other than classical. After nine months, we realized that his gifts were better suited elsewhere and we told him so. Now imagine, only three months previously I had presided at his wedding ceremony. Upon learning that he was dismissed, his new wife sent me anguished letters asking how I could be so callous or call myself a Christian.

Subsequently, we also let go of two administrators and a community worker. This was a very painful period in my ministry. And it was painful for the congregation. I heard and experienced many people's displeasure directly. I got the reputation of being an "axe-man" (not an easy thing considering my "pleaser" personality). Yet these were not unilateral decisions. A team of people, of which I was a member, made each of the decisions, and in doing so acted as leaders.

When Jesus "set his face toward Jerusalem," nobody supported him – not his disciples, not his friends, and certainly not the religious and political authorities. In other words, he had to know from the *inside out* what was necessary. And what he knew was that he had to realize his mission of proclaiming and enacting the kingdom of God; his vision of lifting up the poor, releasing the captives, helping the blind to see and the deaf to hear. He knew that he had an appointment with his destiny and nothing could dissuade him.

I have seen congregations wait ten years to begin a change process because they refused to upset anybody in the congregation with a difficult decision to change staff. I have seen lead ministers leave congregations because the lay leadership team would not deal with a dysfunctional staff member. The church needs leadership that is self-defining, able to stay connected across differences, emotionally intelligent, and shadow-conscious – people who can set their face toward Jerusalem for the sake of the kin-dom of God.

NON-ANXIOUS PRESENCE

These core capacities issue in what Dr. Edwin Friedman calls a "non-anxious presence." This does not mean that we walk around feeling blissed out. It doesn't mean that we've attained a state of enlightenment that elevates us above the fray. It means that we can enter the fray and stay true to ourselves. When everybody is telling us that the sky is falling, we calmly ask for the information that has led them to that apocalyptic conclusion. When somebody tells us that "a lot of people, not just me, are upset," we ask for the names of those people, and then go and talk to them. If the person who is relaying this information is unwilling to give us the names, we calmly tell that person to ask these "unnamed others" to contact us directly. Triangulation – drawing third parties in to deflect the emotional charge of direct communication – is a favourite tactic of undifferentiated people who lack emotional intelligence and self-definition.

What Friedman discovered is that if leaders can stay calm and connected when the system is all in a flap, the system begins to settle down around the leader. Again, being calm does not mean that you don't have feelings. And it doesn't mean going into your office and closing the door behind you so you can meditate. It means going out among those who are upset. It means facing them, listening to them, and being clear with them about your stand on the issue. It means engaging from your deepest, most authentic self. After you've done this, *then* go and meditate! This is inside-out leadership.

At Canadian Memorial, we obviously went through a very chaotic period in the early stages of building our leadership team. Since this tumultuous time, the congregation has more than doubled in size. For the last seven years, we've enjoyed a stable leadership team. The second organist we let go went on to create a world-renowned *a capella* choir and is now organist at a more traditional church. Some people left the congregation and never returned because they thought I was a tyrant and probably still do. I can live with that. It's not the end of the world. It's *never* the end of the world, despite how we might sometimes feel and what our congregation might like us to believe.

Sometimes, of course, I wish I never had the dream of going to Ottawa – of claiming my own seat of power – and I'm still tempted to take the easy way out. Walter Wink calls it the temptation to the "regressive alternative." But on most days my belief in the potential of congregations outweighs my personal fear. I believe we have it within us to make a real difference to a world community in need of healing. Realizing this vision requires leadership.

The Indo-European root of the word leadership, *leith*, means "to go forth," "to cross a threshold," or "to die." Using a biblical metaphor, it is to "set one's face toward Jerusalem" with Christ. Just as Jesus of Nazareth faced into what was most difficult and frightening – his own death by crucifixion – so Christian leaders must be willing to "die with Christ," to use Paul's metaphor. This means letting go of whatever gets in the way of proclaiming and enacting the kin-dom of God. The congregational leader, lay and clergy, must be willing to go forth and cross multiple thresholds. Most often it's the threshold of our own fear – of conflict, of displeasing others, of being self-defined, of staying connected across differences, and of our own disowned shadow. Unless the leader is willing to undergo a death to a timid, play-it-safe self, she or he will never be raised in Christ. It requires courage to set one's face toward Jerusalem. Sometimes it is lonely. Often it is painful. But there is a future that stands in need of us in order to be born – God's future.

MAPPING IT OUT

1. Do a leadership audit. First, make an honest assessment of your ministry staff. Are they working well together? Is this really the team that is going to see you through the next ten years? Are there any "elephants" in the room that people are ignoring because they are too painful or stressful to deal with? Does everybody know that you have a leadership problem, but you find yourself just "waiting it out," hoping the problem person will move on?

2. Do an audit of the health of your lay leadership teams. Do you know who your leaders are? How are you supporting them? Are they being encouraged? What leadership training do you have in place?

[1] C. Otto Scharmer, *Theory U: Leading from the Future as It Emerges* (Cambridge: The Society for Organizational Learning, 2007), 27–47.

[2] Ibid., 7.

[3] Anna S. Christie, *Evoking Change: Make a Difference in Your Life and in the World* (Lincoln, NE: iUniverse, 2007).

nine

Like Living Stones:
The Spiritual Foundations of
Leadership

At daybreak he departed and went to a deserted place.
~ LUKE 4:42 ~

The wise person learns what draws God near –
it is the beauty of compassion in your heart.
~ HAFIZ, SUFI POET ~

Without a solid psychological foundation, the spiritual temple we are building will come tumbling down the moment the enemy stands threatening outside the gate. Once in place, leaders need to attend to the line of development known as spiritual intelligence. What are the foundational spiritual practices for leadership?

The author of 1 and 2 Peter had a compelling vision that inspired him to declare there was no need for a physical temple. The Holy One dwells *within* the believer. Those in Christ are like "living stones" from which the invisible and indestructible spiritual temple of Christ is to be built (1 Peter 2:4–5). As each disciple of Christ connects with this inner life, the future that needs him or her in order to be born may emerge. This is what causes a congregation to light up from within. There are four core spiritual capacities necessary for leadership: stillness, theological reflection, compassion, and creativity.

STILLNESS

In most people, the capacity for stillness is the most underestimated and underdeveloped of the four. Now more than ever in this fast-food, fast-paced, multi-tasking, time-compressed age, we need to learn to be still. I mean by this that we need to learn to stop our minds. The contemplative strand of every religious tradition makes a distinction between the "counterfeit mind" and the Authentic Mind. The counterfeit mind is also known as monkey-mind, because it swings like a monkey from one branch – thought, image, plan, or worry – to another ceaselessly. It also chatters away constantly. We have learned to believe that this counterfeit mind defines us. But it doesn't.

It is possible, by various methods, to calm the mind, to empty it of all thoughts and images, and to rest in an alert yet deeply relaxed state. In so doing, we may achieve what Buddhists call single-mindedness. If we can watch these thoughts and images come and go, what part of us is doing the watching? This is the authentic self. Some would say that when we achieve this empty space we are actually *in* our Christ mind. Others might say that this is the space that forms a bridge to the Christ. It doesn't much matter, as far as I'm concerned. The point is that in this sacred stillness a subtle but radical transformation may occur.

The story of Mary and Martha can be interpreted through this lens (Luke 10:38–42). Martha is miffed that Mary sits "listening" to Jesus instead of helping out with the work. She wants Jesus to order Mary back to her domestic responsibilities. Remarkably, given first-century patriarchal culture, Jesus refuses. He tells Martha that Mary has chosen "the better part."

The better part has nothing to do with the spiritual versus the mundane. After all, Brother Lawrence wrote a book called *Practicing the Presence of God* in which he talks about his kitchen work as his medium of connection with the holy. No, the problem, says Jesus, is that Martha is "distracted and worried by many things" (Luke 10:40). It's not *what* Mary and Martha are doing, but *how* they are doing it. Martha is functioning out of the counterfeit mind, while Mary is pursuing attentively the Authentic Mind. Jesus says that there is only "one thing necessary." I take this to be a reference to the single-mindedness that connects us to the Christ, the generative matrix from which all creativity and the very future emerge.

The authentic state of mind (or no-mind if you prefer) is so transformative because it accomplishes three things in one fell swoop. Otto Scharmer incorporates the language of the late Fransesco Varela into his "Theory U," which addresses organizational change.[1] Descending down the left-hand side of the U we pass through three distinct yet related thresholds. The first he calls suspension. This simply means that we are willing to suspend our take on reality, our worldview, and our assumptions about the nature of the problem we're facing. This is necessary because typically when we try to solve a problem we simply re-enact our habitual ways of seeing the world. The artist Cezanne, practiced what came to be known as "Cezanne's doubt." Before starting to paint, he would intentionally tilt his head in different directions, in order to achieve a new perspective.

Much of what passes for visioning in congregations actually involves merely downloading patterns from the past out of habit. Without suspension, the new thing Spirit is doing through us will never manifest. Stilling the counterfeit or monkey-mind and entering into the Authentic Mind automatically suspends one's take on reality. In fact, my experience is that after a period of this kind of meditation, the way through a previously intransigent problem becomes clear. Scharmer calls this form of intelligence the Open Mind.

Suspension leads to a second movement, as we travel down the left-hand side of the U. This second movement is redirection. Redirection is a subtle process, but we've all experienced it at one time or another. In the normal course of life, we're preoccupied with the in-your-face challenges and problems. We have jobs to do, children to tend, housework to manage, pensions to accumulate. These things occupy the foreground of our awareness. When we stop to still our minds, these temporarily recede to the background and what was background, the Christ Field, becomes foreground. We gain the capacity to see the whole whereas without stillness we can only see the parts. Naturally we confuse the part with the whole. But when we redirect our attention, through stillness – as Mary was doing in Jesus' presence – we see the parts of our lives in the context of a greater whole.

Even more importantly, as we become proficient in the practice of stillness, we gain the capacity to see the whole *within* the various parts of our lives. We are able to practice the presence of God in the midst of our everyday routines and tasks. We understand what Henri Bortoft meant when he said that the "part is the place for the presencing of the whole." Scharmer calls this form of intelligence the Open Heart.

The implications of all this for congregational life are readily apparent. To the extent that we, as disciples of Christ, live with the awareness of Christ – the whole – this awareness will inform both how we live together in community, and the choices we make around mission and programming. Financial and other survivalist concerns (Beige) recede as they are set within the living presence of Christ in our midst. This is the key that ignites the engine of congregational life.

At the bottom of the U is what Varela called "letting go" in order to "let come." We open our *minds* to fresh perspectives through suspension. We open our *hearts* to allow the Christ field to become foreground with redirection. And now, in this phase, we open our *wills* to let go of whatever is standing in the way of the new thing that wants to emerge.

Most vision and mission statements never get far enough down the left-hand side of the U. In fact, they typically engage only the counterfeit mind – thinking *about* good ideas that we might "try out."

Stilling the mind is the most powerful tool we have at our disposal to travel all the way down to the bottom of the U in a way that engages our authentic mind, heart, and will. Scharmer calls the actions that arise after making this journey to the bottom of the U "presencing."

The right-hand side of the U involves acting to put in place what emerges out of these three phases. Any actions that arise at this point transcend decision-making – you just *know* what needs to be done. And the actions are implemented very quickly. At this point in the process, we don't need to engineer them into existence. Rather, we allow them to manifest. Wilfulness gives way to willingness. Scharmer calls this intelligence the Open Will.

As leaders, we need to still our counterfeit mind in order to manifest an open mind, heart, and will. In turn, this openness will allow us to pre-sense, presence, and then enact the sacred emerging future.

THEOLOGICAL REFLECTION

Whereas meditation involves *stilling* the mind in order to connect with the Source, theological reflection involves *focusing* the mind for the same purpose. Congregational leaders have the capacity to set the stories of their lives and their everyday experience within the context of the stories of scripture. They use the language of their tradition to address issues of ultimate concern. Through theological reflection, scripture conveys sacred presence. Our own life experiences become sources of sacred revelation, as we learn to listen deeply to the sacrament that is our life.

There are four meta-narratives, or overarching stories, in the Bible: oppression and liberation, exile and homecoming, sacrifice, and call and response. If we have the capacity for theological reflection, we will naturally talk about our own struggles to overcome addiction, for example, as a story of liberation in which the Holy One yearns for us to be free. We understand our own loneliness and longing to belong as a story that recapitulates the experience of the Jews in exile in Babylonia.

Our longing to hallow what is truly holy and to give ourselves body, mind, and soul to this transcendent cause is validated by the theme of sacrifice throughout scripture. Finally, when our own deep allurements meet the deep needs of the world we name it as a story of divine call.

When our own stories intersect with the stories of scripture, we experience an explosion of meaning and significance. Through theological reflection, we consciously exit the cultural narratives that compete for our allegiance. These tell us that wealth and power, celebrity, and consumerism define the meaning of our lives. Just as the practice of stillness makes what was background – the Christ – foreground, so these cultural narratives recede, making room for an authentic sacred life to emerge.

COMPASSION

Compassion literally means to "suffer with." It is often contrasted with cognition; one has to do with the mind and one with the heart we are told. But it's a false separation. Compassion is the opening of one's heart through the expansion of one's mind. The basis of all authentic love is an increased capacity to take multiple perspectives. The word cognition comes from *co gnosis,* the ability to *know with* another. That is, the ability to see life through the other person's eyes. Without this capacity, love is nothing more than a projection of your own reality onto others. The value systems of Spiral Dynamics represent an evolving capacity to expand the number of perspectives one is able to assume. Love without the ability to take another person's perspective, and validate it, is sentimentality.

A therapist will not be successful unless she is able to join with the client. Until the client trusts that the therapist will know where they are "coming from," without judgment, no change is possible. It's the same for leaders in a congregation. *Until the congregation knows that we care, they won't care how much we know.* The most common error new leaders make is to send messages that say "it's out with the old and in with the new." We'd be much better off to look for all the good work that the congregation has done in the previous 20 or 30 years and then celebrate their initiative and faithfulness. Spend a year digging up stories of the good work that was done before you ever arrived. Praise the good ministry of previous ministers. Don't just show up with your bag full of tricks for creating a new and improved congregation. You'll elicit the same defences any client would throw up having sniffed out that his therapist has an agenda. Appreciation for what has been done by these people before you arrived is compassion in action.

A strange thing happened to me in my fourth year with this congregation. I began to love the people – even the ones who frustrated me. I'd look out over the congregation on a Sunday morning and feel tremendous compassion for the whole lot. Now, I'm not the most "pastoral" of ministers, so I was a little taken aback by this turn of events. But I realized how privileged I was to know the intimate details of what they were all going through. There is so much pain in the pews on any given Sunday morning, and so much joy; so many random and anonymous acts of kindness. There's Joe, who recently wrote a cheque to cover the first and last month's rent of another member who was struggling to make ends meet. Mary, who quietly and unofficially acts as congregational nurse to the elderly, is sitting in her usual pew, as though she's just a regular person and not an angel. Fred was diagnosed with cancer two weeks ago, but he was serving food to the homeless on the weekend.

Yes, there are always those who are infuriating and some days you wish they would just go away. But you find yourself loving even them because we're all just trying to do the best we can. In spite of our wounds and vulnerabilities, and often because of them, we have sitting before us on any given Sunday morning countless unnoticed acts of heroism – triumphs of the human spirit. Once you realize this, your anxiety about your sermon and the logistics of the baptism fade away. It's not about you, after all. Damned if you don't love these people. And if you don't, you've got no business being their leader.

People must trust you before they'll let you lead them. If you don't know them, empathize with them, and flat-out love them, they won't trust you. We've said that leadership happens from the inside out. It's not about techniques. It's not about following a manual or even this book. It's about the interior condition of the leader. And if the leader doesn't love his or her people, then any changes that get made will be merely technical and superficial. Without compassion, a leader begins to *manage* people, in order to get a desired outcome. Information is doled out on an as-needed basis. Secret meetings are held to engineer a vote. Trust is frayed.

CREATIVITY

When most of us hear the word creativity, we think about Mozart, Picasso, Margaret Atwood, or Steven Spielberg. We tend to associate creativity with the arts, and conclude that we are not artistic. Thank God for our artists. I would love to see more congregations become centres for the arts. But this is only one kind of creativity. Scripture records no instances of Jesus writing a poem or creating a painting. Yet he was a virtual centre of creativity. Cosmologically speaking, we can think about Jesus as a kind of second "Fireball." Just as all of creation came flaring forth from the Big Bang, so we believe as Christians that Jesus ushered in a new creation – a new era, a new kingdom, a new way of being human. His creativity was immense!

This kind of creativity is available in more modest forms to all of us. Postmodernism has actually provided us with the key to unlocking our inner creativity and ability to shape new worlds. The secret is being able to assume ever-expanding and more comprehensive perspectives. Recall that the gift of postmodernism is the insight that there is no absolute Truth – only truths that arise in and through context and perspective. To live mythically is to live as though there is only one Truth and to imagine that this Truth is obvious to everybody.

In this sense, we all live in and through myth until we gain the capacity to take a step back and witness our lives *objectively*. This is true at the level of our family of origin, where we unconsciously downloaded our blueprints for what constitutes reality. To evolve, we need to gain perspective on these blueprints, and when we do we are free to shape our lives consciously – a primary act of creativity. This same dynamic holds for the cultural myths and narratives to which we unconsciously offer our allegiance. As we gain perspective, we acquire the capacity to think, act, and live *outside the box*. The box holds the myths and stories that shape our lives.

I recently watched a documentary called *The Garbage Warrior*, which featured architect Michael Reynolds, who has lived in the desert of New Mexico for the last 30 years. Reynolds builds sustainable homes out of the refuse of society – old tires, pop bottles, and discarded refrigerator doors. His homes are built off the power grid. They mimic life processes, in that they take nothing from the earth that doesn't feed the earth.

Thirty years ago, Reynolds stepped outside the dominant cultural myths that tell us human beings are consumers; that the petroleum-based economy is sustainable; that we cannot live away from the energy grid; that pollution and global warming are an inevitable cost of modern civilization; that we must build houses according to accepted architectural models; and that working all your life to pay off a huge mortgage is a sensible life project. For him, these are no more than modern stories we tell ourselves about what constitutes a meaningful life. Reynolds stepped out of the box, looked back at it, and found it very limited. Then he proceeded to become one of the most creative souls I've ever met.

Jesus stepped back and took a look at Caesar's definition of kingdom and simply refused to fit into it. For Jesus, Caesar's kingdom was set within a larger, more comprehensive and more humane kingdom – God's kingdom! Paul met the risen Christ one day and his life gained a new perspective, one that would be oriented around an inside-out love, not religious rules. From this enlarged perspective, he knew that the gospel was for non-Jews as well as for Jews. Then he set about creating a movement among the Gentiles that came to be known as the church. Peter had a dream in the middle of the night that enlarged his perspective on the purity laws of Judaism, which in turn helped him to realize that Paul had been right. Each of these biblical moments was an occasion of blessed creativity.

The church I am most proud of is the one that was able to step outside the box called "church" and realize that women have every bit as much right to be ordained as men, and that excluding certain people from positions of leadership based on their sexual orientation is reprehensible and contrary to the gospel. These days when I preside at the wedding of a gay or lesbian couple, I experience it as the "new thing" God is doing in our day and age. Perspective liberates us to shape a new world, to try new things (even if we fail), and to be the centres of creative emergence that God calls us to be in our congregational life.

The spiritual foundations for leadership are the capacities for stillness, theological reflection, compassion, and creativity. Together with the psychological capacities of staying connected across differences, emotional intelligence, self-definition, and shadow-work, the interior conditions of leadership are set.

DEEPENING THE DEFINITION OF LEADERSHIP

What is a leader? My working definition of leadership derives from Jewish theologian Martin Buber and social scientist Otto Scharmer. A congregational leader is one who has the capacity and willingness to pre-sense and presence the future that needs her congregation in order to emerge. This is, after all, what Jesus did. He *pre-sensed* and then *presenced* the future – what he called the kingdom of God – that needed him and his disciples in order to emerge. The past, present, and the future coalesced in his ministry of proclaiming and enacting the kingdom of God. There is no metaphysical future out there waiting for enough time to elapse before it is realized. God doesn't have a blueprint that we're all just following, and which given enough time will come to pass. We are that part of God – the Body of Christ – that has woken up after 14 billion years and has understood that the future is in our hands. It's time to stop waiting for an external God to intervene. The truth is that God's been waiting for *us*. This inside-out God manifests in those who are willing to be the future present.

MAPPING IT OUT

Develop a comprehensive leadership program for lay leaders. It will pay huge dividends in the long run. Ours is called *Lighting the Way: Training for Leadership*. A group of 12 people covenant to hold each other accountable for psychological and spiritual growth. They know that by taking this program, they are preparing to take leadership positions in the congregation.

You'll need to do screening interviews to make sure that each person has gifts for leadership. It may be that some need to do their own personal therapy before taking this course. I can't emphasize enough the importance of this. It only takes one psychologically or spiritually immature person to radically alter the group dynamic. The other requirement we have is that participants must have taken one of our core Bible study programs.

The leadership-training group meets weekly and is built around the four psychological capacities (emotional intelligence, self-definition, staying connected, and shadow work) as well as the four spiritual capacities (stillness, theological reflection, compassion, and creativity).

Start by teaching meditation practice. The best resource for this that I've come across is Ken Wilber's *Integral Life Practice Kit*.[2] In very simple language, he describes three meditation practices that incorporate three perspectives on Spirit or God. This kit also contains a compassion meditation and a module on working with the shadow. Participants are expected to have a meditation practice throughout the term of the course. This addresses two of the spiritual capacities (stillness and compassion), and one of the psychological capacities (shadow work).

As for the first three core psychological capacities – emotional intelligence, staying connected across differences, and self-definition – it is not possible to teach these capacities if you haven't developed them in yourself. The first step, in this case, is to find your own therapist and dig in. If you feel competent, then use the interpersonal dynamics of the group itself to teach these skills. Typically, congregations function at a very superficial level. This is a great opportunity to help people go deep within the safety of a group facilitated by a skilled leader. As trust deepens, people will trigger each other. There will be plenty of opportunity to help people identify their feelings – mad, sad, glad, afraid, and ashamed are the essential ones. Can they take responsibility for their own feelings? Help them to share authentically with each other what is surfacing for them. Can they stay connected across differences of opinions, values, and beliefs? It's going to get real. That's the point. Teach them about triangulation. Gossip was destructive in the early church and it's equally deadly in 21st-century congregations. Model a different way yourself. Listen to nobody who tells you what another person told her about you or anybody else. Just say no.

Use a Spirit-given gift inventory (and other tools such as the Myers-Briggs inventory and the Enneagram) to help participants identify their gifts for ministry and where they intend to serve within the congregation. We are developing teaching modules for worship leadership (including preaching and leading prayers), ministry team leadership (if they have a specific ministry in mind), core team leadership, audio-visual team leadership, and many others.

At the end of the year, have a spiritual retreat and then commission your leaders to their chosen areas of ministry in a service of worship.

Finally, teach a model of theological reflection, using weekly lectionary readings. Here's a simple but very effective model that my wife, Dr. Ann Evans, developed.

1. Begin with an experience. It should be one that feels like a cloud that follows you around. The fact that it stays with you is an indication that there is spiritual gold to be mined and lessons to be learned. Write a case study about it, describing it in detail.

2. Think of a scriptural story or teaching that reminds you of your experience. Set your experience within the context of one or more of the lectionary readings for the upcoming Sundays, or choose one of the four meta-narratives of scripture and reflect on your experience within this framework.

3. Symbolize this experience through some kind of creative expression. Write a poem, sing a song, dance, bake brownies, sculpt with some clay, paint a picture. By doing so, you validate your experience as sacred, as a way in which the Holy One is communicating with you. You also ground the experience in that, in many instances, you will be left with an artifact that will always remind you of the gracious way Spirit spoke to you. Finally, it ensures that your theological reflection is not composed of all right-brain activity. Each week, have a different member share their theological reflection.

4. Teach the group the dos and don'ts of offering feedback. The question is not whether they liked the reflection or not. Rather, help them focus on and stay with what the reflection did *for them*. Do not let them offer any correction.

Here's a possible format for such a group.

Light a Christ candle. Begin with a 20-minute silent meditation. Have the person assigned to be the week's presenter do their theological reflection, along with their creative expression (20 minutes). Follow this with group feedback on the reflection. Focus on what the reflection brought up in the listeners. This is not a critique. Ask clarifying questions. Offer gratitude. This takes the first hour of the group.

Begin the second hour with a check-in. We call this time "highs and lows." The fancy name in our tradition is *consolation* and *desolation*. When finished, invite the group to talk about what is going on inside of them in the moment. The group will now move into interpersonal dynamics. Whatever emerges will be used to teach about the core psychological capacities required for leadership – self-defining, staying connected across differences, taking responsibility for one's own feelings, and the shadow-work of withdrawing unconscious negative projections. Close with five minutes of silence.

---

[1] C. Otto Scharmer, *Theory U: Leading from the Future as It Emerges* (Cambridge: The Society for Organizational Learning, 2007).

[2] Ken Wilber, *Integral Life Practice: Version 1.0*, Boulder: The Integral Life Institute, 2006). Order at www.integralinstitute.org.

ten

The Too Heavy Task:
The Perils of Pastoral
Visitation

What you are doing is not good.
You will surely wear yourself out, both you and
these people with you.
For the task is too heavy for you; you cannot do it alone...

~ EXODUS 18:17–23, SPOKEN BY JETHRO, MOSES' FATHER-IN-LAW ~

Please come for a visit, our committee sure needs you;
My uncle Tom's in the hospital and
Mrs. Avery is feeling blue,
Charlie's feeling left out, he's our Randall Hurst;
So get it straight who's got the pull; in this place the first
shall be first.

~ *BURNOUT*, BRUCE SANGUIN ~

What I am about to say may be the most important thing in this book. The number of people any individual can authentically hold in his heart and effectively care for is around ten or 12. Where did we ever get the idea that one individual – the minister or the pastor – can be the primary caregiver of an entire congregation? I know. We are ordained, at least in my denomination, to the ministry of Word, Sacrament, and *Pastoral Care*. This has been interpreted in the past to mean that we end up being every member's personal chaplain. It is perhaps the most destructive assumption about what ordained ministry is about, and it needs to go away.

For one thing, it's not possible. I spent the first ten years of ministry either trying to be everybody's personal chaplain, or feeling guilty that I wasn't doing a good job of it. Either way, it's a recipe for burnout. There is always somebody we haven't visited, another who has ended up in the hospital, yet somebody else who needs pastoral counselling. It can literally drive you crazy thinking about it – and it *does* drive some clergy crazy. I look around at too many of my colleagues and see ashen faces and joyless demeanours. Now, I'm not laying this all at the feet of the ministry of "visitation." But a good bit of clergy burnout can be attributed to the assumptions we have about how ordained persons should fulfill their responsibilities for pastoral care.

Second, pastoral care is the single biggest reason why congregations are stuck. Culture shifting requires immense energy and leadership. The inertia built up in many congregations is significant. Turning the ship, or at least redirecting it, often requires every bit of available energy, and more. Somehow – and I'll talk about how below – congregations need to get their ordained leadership out of the role of personal chaplain. That is, they need to do this if they are interested in becoming an emerging congregation. But if you're reading this book, then you're interested in making a culture shift. Write the following sentence down somewhere:

> *The role of clergy needs to shift from personal chaplain*
> *to spiritual leader and equipper of the saints in Christ.*

FROM PERSONAL CHAPLAIN TO SPIRITUAL LEADER

When I came to Canadian Memorial, I told the search committee, and I quote, "*I don't do tea.*" Yes, this is partly because I'm not the world's greatest visitor. I admit it. But in my first 10 years of ministry, I had my fill of innocuous "visits," photo album sessions, and tea. I also enjoyed delightful visits, filled with meaningful conversations and exceptional tea! But too often my pastoral visits would follow one of two predictable patterns.

I found the first pattern the most frustrating. The primary purpose of the visit in this scenario is to feed the dynamic that will ensure future visits. Let me explain. It all starts with the obligatory visit from the minister and the need to register that this has happened. Well, it registers. Word circulates, which of course sets up a dynamic whereby others wonder when they will get *their* visit, or why they haven't already been visited. I noticed that on many of these visits the elderly would write out a cheque for their monthly contribution. They had "gotten behind" a few months, but perhaps I could take this to the church for them. That's when it clicked what these visits were about historically. They were part of a co-dependent system of rewards and privileges – specifically, the privileges that come with "membership." Their offering acted as a reward for visiting them. The minister could expect the same thing during the next visit. The visit was a ritual that gave the member power and that ensured the minister would stay on the hamster wheel.

In the second pattern, we would make small talk for 45 minutes. I would announce that I should probably be going, and then the "visitee" would tell me, as I was walking out the door, that they had just been diagnosed with cancer. No, they didn't have any family in town – an aging sister, but she can't drive anymore. So I would turn around and have a fourth cup of tea.

Even as my heart ached for these poor souls, I couldn't help but realize that I had just added to my ever-expanding pastoral care circle. This is part of the dysfunction of the model of clergy as personal chaplain. The more compassion we extend, the more our workload increases. The more involved we get in the life of our families, the larger our span of care becomes. This is the paradox set up by the model of clergy as personal chaplain.

Making the shift from clergy as personal chaplain to clergy as spiritual leader and equipper of the saints in Christ is perhaps the most difficult part of becoming an emergent congregation. I have seen too many congregations push out into the sea of culture shifting only to run aground on the shoals of visitation ministry. Visitation has been part of the prevailing culture for hundreds of years, and it won't change without intentional focus. If you are a clergyperson reading this, trying to figure out what battles are worth fighting, put this one at the top of your list. If you are a lay leader, I recommend sorting this out as soon as possible.

A congregation can find a hundred ways to sabotage this shift: an innocent phone call from an elder of the congregation inquiring whether you've visited her friend recently; murmuring in the coffee hour after the service and in the church parking lot after meetings. People who never miss a Sunday will be conspicuous by their absence and somebody will inevitably ask if they've had a visit recently. (To which the appropriate response is, "I'm not sure. Have they received a *congregational* visit recently?" The real question being asked, of course, is whether *the minister* has visited these people lately.) Or maybe the chair of finance will note that givings are down over last year – and they may well be. (Again, you might ask, "So what is *the congregation* going to do about these people who are withholding their money as leverage?") Whatever the tactic, don't give in.

The requirement that the minister act as personal chaplain to the congregation is the most co-dependent, dysfunctional vestige of the age of Christendom we continue to contend with. It takes two to tango, though, doesn't it?

The second source of sabotage comes from clergy themselves. Despite the fact that we've been run ragged for decades and may be bereft of any spiritual juice or discernible passion for life, we often cling to this role. We love to believe that we are indispensable. So we buy into the silly assumption that only a visit from the minister "counts" as a real visit. It inflates our ego. We're really very important. We're great listeners. All compassion resides in us.

In our more rational moments, we don't listen to this voice. We understand that it's the part we play in propping up a sick system. Naturally, we care as much as the next person. I continue to visit people in the hospital and when a pastoral emergency arises I want to be present. But we need to let go of the traditional model of pastoral visitation before we try to make a culture shift.

THE INVISIBLE NETWORK OF PASTORAL CARE

There exists in every congregation an informal and invisible network of pastoral caregivers. Point this out to the congregation and validate it! The living Christ resides in every one of these visitors. They wouldn't call it "pastoral care," of course. Nothing so highfalutin as that! They're just lending a helping hand, driving a friend to a cancer treatment, making a casserole for somebody going through a difficult time, helping somebody move to a care centre. It's nothing much, they believe. But in fact, they are the Body of Christ and when they are validated in this way, they light up. Their visiting *counts!* People in the emerging congregation take care of one another.

There are lots of wonderful pastoral visitation programs out there, such as Stephen's Ministry. But a word of caution. Too often, these programs get implemented without first deconstructing the model of clergy as personal chaplain. That expectation is left in place, only now the minister gets some *help* with *his* job. Still, these programs are a godsend when both the clergy and the congregation have let go of the old paradigm.

Some congregations hire a retired minister to do the visiting, which can work in certain situations. But if the old model is still operative, this will be little more than a strategy for helping out the lead minister. She will still be expected to visit.

At Canadian Memorial, we were blessed with a large constituency of elderly people, many of whom held this assumption about the role of clergy when I arrived. Realistically, we couldn't just go cold turkey. Through our Spirit-given gifts process, we identified a woman who was gifted in pastoral care. We hired her to help with the transition away from the old model. We made it clear that her primary role was to focus on the aging demographic. But we also made it clear that she was going to deconstruct that old passive model, whereby "seniors" are always on the receiving end of visits. We saw no reason why these competent and compassionate souls could not form networks of care among themselves, since only a very small percentage found themselves in circumstances whereby they couldn't be pastoral caregivers to each other.

Kay, at age 89, helped us to rewrite our Spirit-given gifts inventory. Helen, who has been in a wheelchair all of her life and who lost the use of her limbs to a disease in childhood, learned to paint by holding a brush in her teeth. She makes "get well" cards for the sick. Others, who are able to knit, make prayer shawls for those who are undergoing chemotherapy treatment. Some write exquisite thank you cards.

Honour and validate existing networks of care.

SMALL GROUP MINISTRY

The most effective way to deconstruct the old paradigm and to create an alternative is through small group ministry. By small group ministry I mean something specific. I do not mean small numbers of people who get together to do some task or even to study together. There are legions of these kinds of groups doing great ministry and study together. We call these groups *ministry teams*. We have approximately 35 of them at Canadian Memorial.

Small group ministry, as I use the term, refers to something different. It's an intentional program that begins with the training of lay leaders who then seek out others to form small groups of ten to 12 people. Together, the people in these groups build spiritual friendships, reflect on the weekly scripture readings, pray for each other, and do some kind of outreach program as a group. Each group meets once every couple of weeks, either at the home of the leader or at the church. Their sessions last 90 minutes. This time is divided into two periods: 45 minutes for scriptural reflection, and 45 minutes for personal sharing and upholding one another in prayer.

An amazing thing happens when you put human beings together in a group. They start to care for one another. Remember the biological principle of self-organization, whereby life just knows how to do life? Small group ministry is an example of creating a structure that mimics nature's own processes, where we see natural grace at work. If somebody is having a tough time with a teenage son or daughter, the group naturally finds ways to gather between small group meetings to offer support. If one member ends up in the hospital, the others visit. This caring is an emergent dynamic. It just happens spontaneously from within the group. The leaders of the group will naturally let me know if somebody is going through a difficult time – *if* they have the permission of that person. But they won't tell me about it so that I can take care of the situation. The group takes care of the person. I mean this. Clergy are not required to do pastoral care for those who participate in these small groups. It would be weird and offensive, in fact, if I started to butt in.

Each group has two co-leaders. These people are given training sessions a few times a year. They learn how to do theological reflection, pray for another person, how to listen, and the basics of group dynamics theory. Notice that the span of care is ten to 12 people. Group leaders act as shepherds or mentors for the participants. They have a heart especially for the newcomers in the group. Where is the newcomer in their faith journey? Do they need Bible study, a meditation group, or a spiritual gifts seminar? Are they ready to take a membership class? Small group leaders mentor the participants in their Christian journey.

When the group grows beyond 12 members, it births another group. One of the co-leaders takes a few of the existing group and begins another group. This norm of birthing is difficult for many groups, but it is essential because it signals that these groups are completely open to newcomers and that their reason for being is not the warm and fuzzy feelings group members develop for each other over time, although this happens. The groups are meant to be mission-oriented. We exist for others. Thus, groups leave an open chair for anybody who might need the caring circle of the group in his or her life, and they actively seek out new members for the group.

Still, the temptation to close the circle is strong, and it has happened a couple of times at Canadian Memorial. Frankly, I don't think it's healthy. Congregational growth consultant and author Bill Easum once said that "new life comes to us on the way to someone else." This mission orientation is what keeps groups from stagnating, as they open themselves to the influence of new members. In an emergent paradigm, the new members are the "parts" that will result in a new whole.

Besides becoming the foundation of pastoral care in a congregation, small group ministry has other side benefits. People learn to pray publicly for one another in the groups. At Canadian Memorial, when we want to open a meeting with prayer, people no longer have to turn to the minister. Some people do this instinctually, but I then simply ask if anybody else would be willing to lead the prayers and usually someone steps up. It seems like a small thing, but it's a sign of spiritual maturity.

It's also a sign that leadership is being shared. In training your small group leaders, you are doing very effective leadership development. These people begin to take ownership of their identity as spiritual leaders of the congregation.

Small group ministry is also the most effective way I've found for integrating newcomers into the life of the congregation. Church growth research shows that if a newcomer doesn't make a significant connection with four or five other people within the first six weeks of coming to church, they won't join with the congregation.

Interestingly, the same dynamic applies to people with a much longer history with the congregation. The truth is, people in small groups come to church on Sundays more regularly. The reason is simple. They look forward to seeing and being with their friends. A while ago, we went through a period of letting small group ministry slip, when our coordinator decided that she wanted a new challenge. There was a noticeable drop in attendance during that year, and I'm convinced that it had to do with the falling off of our small groups.

Finally, small groups are the most natural way to ease the pastoral visitation task that is too heavy for any individual.

There are all kinds of small groups and no single model is the "correct" one. For example, there are affinity groups, in which people with similar interests get together, and there are small groups that have a curriculum of study as a component. We are experimenting with small groups based on the 12-Step program for persons in recovery from addiction. The program is called "12 Steps As Spiritual Journey." The steps work very well as a spiritual practice for all persons, not just those in recovery from addiction. Whatever model is used, it's important that the group have an interpersonal component. People need to form spiritual friendships.

At Canadian Memorial, we are also teaming up with a movement called *Be the Change* (www.bethechangeearthalliance.org), brought to Vancouver by Maureen Jack-Lacroix. These are support groups that help participants make measurable lifestyle changes to lighten our ecological footprint. This focus fits well within a creation-centred paradigm. Our intention is to start these at Canadian Memorial and then help these groups spring up in other congregations and denominations.

Small group ministry is the most effective way I know of getting out of the way of the congregation doing what comes naturally for friends of Christ – caring for one another, holding each other in prayer, and becoming spiritual friends. I cannot guarantee that making this shift will be easy. It took a lot of resolve to stick with the plan and a few years to help the congregation understand that pastoral visitation is a ministry of all the people. When a small group participant is going through a rough patch, instead of having one person to provide care, she will have ten people from the congregation to rally around her and give her the strength she needs to prevail.

MAPPING IT OUT

1. Clarify the existing assumptions in your congregation about pastoral visitation by having a conversation with your Think Tank and your board. Introduce the idea of having the congregation take ownership of pastoral visitation as their responsibility.

2. Now have a conversation about freeing your minister's time from being personal chaplain to being the spiritual leader of the culture shift and the equipper of the saints in Christ.

3. Identify the people who constitute the invisible and informal network of pastoral care that already exists in your congregation. Invite them to a luncheon and have each person tell the story of who they visit. Honour the work they are doing as the very presence of the Christ in your midst. Talk with them about the change you are considering and how they may play a critical role.

4. Find a lay leader to coordinate this network, or hire someone to oversee this ministry.

5. Now go out and find your first two small group leaders. If you are using a Spirit-given gifts inventory, they should have the gifts of leadership, shepherding/mentorship, and hospitality. They should also be biblically literate.

6. Ideally, one of these first small group leaders will be willing to be the small group ministry coordinator when the number of groups begins to multiply. Having a coordinator, lay or clergy, will be pivotal to the success of small groups.

7. Four times a year have a training and support workshop for small group leaders. (One of my colleagues in ministry reviews the lectionary scripture readings with the small group leaders once a month.)

eleven

Eggs or Scorpions?
The Ministry of Hospitality

Is there anyone among you who, if your child asks for an egg,
will instead give a scorpion?
If you then, who are evil, know how to give good gifts to
your children,
how much more will the heavenly Father give the Holy
Spirit to those who ask him!

~ LUKE 11:12–13 ~

Newcomers step across the threshold of our congregations in fear and trembling. They bring with them trepidation and anticipation in equal measure – trepidation because entering any new community is fraught with dangers and insecurities; anticipation because the reason they're coming in the first place is to receive the Holy Spirit.

They would never use that language of course. More likely they would say that they got up this morning and something compelled them to try church again. What the world offered them has come up short. They asked for an egg and they got a scorpion; asked for a fish and were handed a snake. It happens all the time. Now they want to know what it means to be "rich toward God" (Luke 12:21). The pursuit of wealth and security is wearing thin. They come to us more desperate than they often know themselves. It is a common occurrence for one of these souls in exile to weep through their first four or five experiences of worship. They can't tell you why exactly: perhaps a loved one died and this is the anniversary of their death, or the service triggered memories of attending church as a child. But go deeper and you'll find a deep longing for the Holy Spirit. They've been in the wilderness chasing after other gods that have not delivered on their promises. They come with such vulnerable hope.

I am filled with compassion for these seekers. Many of them literally just show without a clue as to what kind of church they've walked into. They could have ended up in some kind of Jim Jones cult. They've been walking through a desert and many of them don't know how to distinguish between a mirage and an oasis. We rarely appreciate their vulnerability. What does it mean to offer them a cold drink of water, something to eat, and a place to rest their wandering souls? In Bedouin cultures, a stranger is offered the absolute best food available. The Bedouins know that in the geography of the desert, lives depend upon their hospitality. Our culture has proven to be a desert for many who show up on Sunday morning. They are parched for Spirit, and what they have an eye out for, more than anything else, is whether the Spirit lives within this community of people. They hope against hope that this is a place where people have asked the "Father" for the gift of the Holy Spirit, and can help them to open to the gift as well. This is the ministry of hospitality – the offering of the Spirit of God to those in exile.

There is a reason I put this chapter near the end of the book and not at the beginning. Too many denominations and too congregations *begin and end* their attempts at culture shifting with hospitality, often interpreted as welcoming newcomers. Greeters are trained to ask the right questions, to direct traffic, and to make sure nobody stands alone in coffee hour. Calls are made to follow up with first-time visitors.

Having a system for welcoming and following up with newcomers is indeed very important. But it's only the beginning, and it puts the cart before horse. It also trivializes hospitality. It doesn't matter how "warm and welcoming" we perceive ourselves to be (and in my experience we think we're more welcoming than we actually are). If we haven't done the difficult work of shifting our culture in preparation to receive these newcomers – in other words, if the Spirit is not animating the life of the congregation, if it's not lighting up disciples from within – the flashiest greeter program in the world won't do much good. And it actually misrepresents the congregation.

Too many denominations and congregations over-promise and under-deliver when it comes to their newcomer programs and the core ministry of conveying the Holy Spirit. Offering a double-shot of Starbucks espresso in the narthex before the service signals that we're hip; and sure, it's fun. But offering a double-portion of the Spirit is our business. Don't confuse culture-shifting – moving from a membership paradigm to a discipleship paradigm; from a redemption focus to a creation-centred focus; from a pastoral care model that demands that clergy function as personal chaplains to a model based on small group ministry; from seeing the role of the laity as *helping out* the minister to implementing the spiritual principle of *ministry anywhere, anytime, by anybody*; from asking people to serve on committees, to inviting them to participate in spiritual-gifts-based ministry; from a bureaucracy of mistrust to a bureaucracy of trust (more on this in the next chapter) – don't confuse these culture-shifting changes with what amounts to a training program for greeters.

A greeter's program has a proper place within an overall *culture* of hospitality, where Spirit lights it up from the inside out. Newcomers are asking for an egg. Let's make them an omelette.

With that rather impassioned caveat in place, I offer the essential elements of a comprehensive hospitality program. (Obviously, if you're just getting started with shifting your culture, you aren't going to wait three years before treating newcomers hospitably. My caution is about implementing a greeter program as a *substitute* for the culture shift.)

WORSHIP – FROM BEGINNER'S MIND

Worship is not the only entry point into a congregation. In fact, an emergent congregation intentionally cultivates multiple entry points. But worship remains a key point of access for the newcomer. It's important, therefore, to do an audit of what happens on Sunday morning with beginner's mind – a Buddhist practice of intentionally perceiving the familiar world of form and structure with a new mind.

Remember the movement down the left-hand side of the U that has to do with suspension? Well, try to suspend all your assumptions: that you are warm and welcoming; that everybody knows they are welcome; that your worship service is accessible; that everybody loves to sing (lots of people don't).

Most of us have access to denominational resources that focus on greeting newcomers and most of these are well done. Therefore, I'll be brief.

The worst question in the history of greeter ministry: "Are you new with us?" Ban the question. Chances are the person has been coming for six months – the last time the greeter who asked the question was on duty. I simply say, "I'm sorry if we were introduced before, but I've forgotten your name."

The worst thing you can hand a newcomer: a shoddy, unprofessionally prepared newcomer's package. Throw it out, today. Do an audit of all your printed materials. They should reflect your vision, mission, and values. If they don't, get rid of them and spend some money on new resources.

If newcomers arrive with a baby, make sure to tell them where the nursery is and that there are change tables available – change tables *are* available, right? Then escort them to the nursery. If they arrive with older children, let them know that they are welcome at Sunday school and where the washrooms are located.

Oh yeah. Be friendly. Your greeter team should be composed of people whom you would like to be greeted by if you walked into a strange community. In my last congregation, one of the greeters had the nasty habit of pushing his false teeth out of his mouth with his tongue before handing people the bulletin. I insisted that he employ his spiritual gifts elsewhere. Yes, he'd been doing it for 15 years. Yes, his feelings were hurt. And yes, he found a different place to serve, where he didn't scare unsuspecting visitors.

Truly, this is not rocket science. Many newcomers literally have not been to church before. Therefore, assume nothing. Don't be clubby. Our minister of music introduces himself every time he stands up to teach a new hymn. It drives a few of our old-timers crazy. But he's using beginner's mind. Take a look at your order of service, if you use one. Remove words like narthex and transept, and if you use the Lord's Prayer, print it in the order of service. Trust me, people who are younger than 40 don't know it. Help people to know when they're supposed to stand and sit. If you're doing a Communion service, explain the drill, exactly what they're supposed to do and say, and make sure you tell them that they're welcome. Don't tell them that Communion will be by "intinction" – the only thing this communicates to newcomers is that they need a dictionary to belong to this church. Tell them to take the bread and dip it in the juice, say amen, and then put it in their mouth and eat it.

The opening words of welcome by the worship presider are important. They set the tone and signal what people are in for. People will already have picked up a lot of information just by the way they were greeted. Impressions are beginning to form. When the guy wearing the long white dress stands up to speak, the newcomer's antennae are really tuned in. If the greeting is staid and formal, it speaks volumes. Get out from behind the lectern to welcome the congregation. This is an opportunity to signal to newcomers that you're thrilled they've chosen to be with you, and why you exist as a congregation. It may provide their first inclination that the Spirit they've been asking for, either directly or indirectly, can be found in this oasis.

My greeting goes like this:

Welcome. If you're a newcomer, we're thrilled that you've chosen to be with us this morning. Please come and have coffee or tea following the service. We'd love to get to know you better. We're a community that exists to teach an expansive and inclusive Christian faith, to act for peace, and to nurture loving community. We meet together in small groups to support one another and to hold each other in prayer. You are welcome to join one of these groups. Look for anybody wearing an "Ask Me about Small Groups" button. May the Spirit of God richly bless you this morning.

I learned an important lesson from reading Alice Walker's novel *The Color Purple*. Shug, a blues singer who's been around the block a few times, informs her young, naïve friend Celia that everything she ever learned about God she brought *with* her into church. Let's honour this insight in the way we do the Call to Worship. I walk out into the congregation and ask what spiritual wisdom they bring with them this morning. I hand people the microphone and they share how Spirit has been active in their lives in the past week. It's a loud and clear sign to newcomers that Spirit is alive and well in this place, and that each of us is a "living stone" radiating with the presence of Spirit. In this same spirit, our Prayers of the Community happen in one of two ways: either I go out and ask for their personal prayers, repeating them back so the congregation can hear; or lay people, trained to write and deliver the prayers, lead them.

When we come to Sharing the Peace of God, our sanctuary lights up. People leave the pews and embrace one another. Typically, I need to interrupt the love in order to get on with the service. While extreme introverts may find this intimidating, most newcomers "feel the love." It's what they came for and here they see it in action. Our sharing of the peace in this way did not happen overnight. It was part of our culture shift. As well as having liturgical integrity – making peace with one another, as Jesus taught, before making our offering – it emerged as a natural outgrowth of the life of discipleship we've been sharing for years.

Sermons matter. My denomination went through a period during which we tried to downplay the importance of the sermon. We didn't want to believe that the interior condition of our leaders – reflected clearly and publicly in preaching – was important. What about the priesthood of *all* believers? Well, that's true, and we all have special Spirit-given gifts for service, but if the preacher can't preach, your church won't thrive. There, I said it. The preacher embodies the congregation's vision, mission, and values. The unique way that God calls this community of faith to be the Body of Christ emerges through her. She carries the morphic field of the congregation – she's in regular communication with the angel of the congregation.

What I'm about to say should be obvious, but apparently it isn't, so here goes. If sermons are boring, something is desperately wrong with the interior condition of the preacher. A congregation shouldn't tolerate this. More importantly, if hospitality means offering the Holy Spirit to souls wandering in the desert, a boring sermon is like giving people a scorpion (which they can find in abundance in the desert). Sermons should be authentic. I learned in seminary that we should keep our own stories and our own lives out of the sermon. Nonsense. Of course, we shouldn't leave people with the impression that they need to rescue us, but they should get a sense that we inhabit the same planet as they do. Share your pain, your ecstasy, your questions, your doubts, and your passion. If you find yourself in the wilderness spiritually, then convey what that is like as honestly as possible, and bring the gospel to bear on the geography of desolation. Yes, sermons should convey passion. The medium really is the message. If the preacher gives the impression that he's bored, why should anybody listen?

Recently, I found myself at a reunion with my siblings dancing wildly to Guns and Roses, after a little too much wine. Over the music I shouted, "Don't move till you feel the groove," which broke us all up. But I wanted us to feel the music from the inside. I know that a sermon I'm preparing is worthwhile if it actually moves me emotionally. Prime the pump before writing a sermon. Turn on your favourite music, go for a walk by the ocean or in the forest, read sacred poetry, pray, dance ecstatically – whatever it takes to get some holy feeling going. *Don't write till you feel the light!*

Finally, the sermon should be *good* news. I learned in seminary from theologian Karl Barth that the great preachers wrote their sermons with the Bible in one hand and the newspaper in the other. Take this with a grain of salt. Of course, be relevant. Address the issues of the day. But the media creates an image of the world at its absolute worst. Over the past few decades, the crime rate has actually gone down in North America – and fairly dramatically at that – but you would never know it from watching the evening news. The world is not as bad as we like to make it out to be, and if our sermons consistently convey that Christ is *against* culture, we'll miss the important truth that Christ is also found *in* culture. Hospitality means that people should leave a service with a little more hope than they brought with them.

MUSIC

We've all been around the block a few times with music in our services – traditional or contemporary, organ or worship band? The answer, not surprisingly, is yes. I've tried blended worship and I've tried creating two services, one with more traditional music and one with more contemporary music. The problem is that I was wrong in many of my assumptions. Many of our elderly people loved the new music and the worship band (if you're using drums, throw away the sticks and get some brushes). When we went to a second service, they missed it. By the same token, many of our younger people are nostalgic for the music they remembered when they attended church 20 years ago, and so missed the organ in the "contemporary" service. Furthermore, many newcomers tell me that they don't like singing – any form of singing. They go mute when the singing starts. Sheesh!

At Canadian Memorial, we're back to a blended format. Balance is the rule. We're blessed with a music minister who loves classical music, composes for orchestras, but then plays keyboard and drums with our worship band. We go from gospel to pop/rock, to traditional, to *Taizé* chants. Quality control is the key, whatever the form.

Music moves the soul. When a solo or a hymn clicks with the theme of the service, magic happens. I hate to admit it, but long after people forget what the sermon was about, they're still humming the music. The key here is to focus on *congregational* singing. This is not primarily a performance. Sacred music is about helping the heart open to the Holy – making a joyful noise unto our God. Therefore, the worship band, the choir, and the music leaders need to focus on enabling the congregation to sing their faith with gusto and with passion. They are worship leaders, not performers.

Incidentally, a worship band and a choir are wonderful entry points into a church community. We call our staff person in charge of the music program a Minister of Music, rather than a Music Director. We think that this title conveys the pastoral and spiritual dimension of leadership implicit in the position. We expect our music minister to be a spiritual leader; to convey our vision, mission, and values; and to be conscious that the music ministry is an entry point. In times past, our choirs formed a very tight clique and were composed of those who liked the musical training and the performance aspect of the choir, but who otherwise had little to do with the life of the congregation. Today, we want our choir members and band members to intentionally offer their Spirit-given gifts in the service of worship. Our choir is now in the habit of sitting in the pews with the rest of the congregation for the sermon. It signals that they are spiritual pilgrims just like the rest of the congregation.

Worship is sacred ritual intended to pry open the door of our hearts to the Holy Spirit. It is our greatest opportunity to show sacred hospitality to the stranger. This is the litmus test. Our sacred rituals convey more powerfully than anything else in the life of the community our inner radiance in Christ – or lack thereof.

NEWCOMER'S LUNCHEONS

Once a month we invite anybody who feels like a newcomer to stay for lunch after the service. It doesn't matter if they've been coming for six months. If they still feel like a newbie, they're welcome. These luncheons have become a mainstay of our ministry of hospitality. Along with our staff, core representatives from our ministry teams attend. Over lunch, we go around the circle and share how we found Canadian Memorial, where we are in our spiritual journey, and a couple of life passions. We share our own stories of Canadian Memorial.

Most importantly, we ask everyone attending the luncheon why they came to Canadian Memorial. Here's what they say. Our signs. Our website. Because they received a personal invitation. The sermons. The music.

And why do they stick around? The opportunity for spiritual friendship and spiritual practice. You can build a hospitality program around these responses. I've already mentioned sermons, music, and small group ministry, so I'll briefly address the other areas.

Signs

We have two signboards, both located on busy city streets. We change the message each week. The least effective thing you can do with these signs is display the title of the sermon and who's preaching. Nobody cares. The second least effective thing you can do with them is advertise upcoming events – unless the Dalai Lama or some other famous person is visiting. Trust me: nobody cares about your potluck supper or garage sale.

The most effective thing you can do is collect short, pithy sayings that reflect the theology and vision and mission of your congregation. Most resources that contain sayings for church signs are pretty lame:

"Prevent Truth Decay, Brush Up On Your Bible." Bada boom. But our most recent saying – "The mind is like a parachute. It only works when it's open" – conveys the ethos and the culture of the congregation. Open-mindedness is not typically associated with the Christian church.

Signs with sayings like these act like Jesus' parables – they're a little bit disorienting. I want our signs to help break down the public stereotypes of what it means to be Christian. People in the community call the church office if we've forgotten to change the sign. They're paying attention. Believe me, this sign ministry is effective. As I said above, newcomers have told us that it was one of the primary reasons they decided to check us out.

Website

People love our website. We've been fortunate to have wonderful web-masters who have donated their time to develop and maintain it. The website reflects our vision, mission, and values, and has all the information anybody could ever want about life at Canadian Memorial. It's not flashy. It's easy to get around. My sermons are posted on the website. We have created a virtual community composed of people from all across North America who read the sermons and contact us. By the time this book is released, all the sermons will be available in audio-visual pod cast. The website is an entry point for a whole community of seekers within and beyond the city of Vancouver. In the context of hospitality, it should convey Spirit.

E-Newsletter

Create an e-newsletter. It saves trees and it's less labour-intensive than a print version. For a modest price, there are many companies that will walk you through the process of creating a professional looking template (see for example, www.constantcontact.org). It's worth the expense. Have a sign-up sheet at the office, the worship service, and on the website for any visitors who would like to receive the newsletter. Grow your e-mail lists in any way you can, with permission of course. Like a website, an e-newsletter can create a virtual community. The headings for the template should reflect your vision, mission, and values.

Bring a Friend

Are your people inviting friends to come to church? This is the front line of hospitality. Personal invitations work. Research shows that people are far more disposed to give church half a chance, if invited by a personal friend. For one thing, they have somebody to sit with in church who will introduce them to other people.

If you're not extending invitations to friends and family, why not? Is there something you're doing, or not doing, that would help them overcome their reticence? Make the last Sunday of every month "Bring a Friend to Church Sunday." If your worship service is consistently high quality, you won't need to do anything spiffy or roll out the red carpet. Just offer the Spirit.

Create Multiple Entry Points

Mission is one of the most effective ways to attract and integrate newcomers. We have many people, including the husbands of women in our congregation, who wouldn't be caught dead in church, but who show up to feed the homeless. In doing so, they discover Christian community. A group that gathers to make sandwiches on Saturday for street kids, called Street Meals, is an entry point for others. An environmental team plans a major conference called "Green Homes and Green Churches – Families for Earth." Our Peace Team sponsors a play about WW II. All of these represent significant entry points for newcomers.

Within an emergent paradigm, mission can happen from the inside-out, originating from within our own congregations. Richard and William are members of Canadian Memorial who are challenged by mental health issues. They sit in the front pew every Sunday morning and are loved by the congregation. Some time ago, the Health Authority changed the regulations relating to their housing, which meant they would be forced to relocate to another home. As a result, they faced the possibility of losing both their church community and the community with whom they shared a home. During announcements one Sunday morning, Richard stood up and shared with us his fears about the move. A team of people, led by our minister of pastoral care, started to lobby on Richard and William's behalf. After many meetings, phone calls, and e-mails, they were allowed to stay in their home. This was justice work – being a voice for the voiceless – from the inside-out.

Baptisms and Weddings

Over the years, my position on baptisms and weddings has softened considerably. Because of the beauty of our sanctuary, many couples want to get married at Canadian Memorial. Each of these couples is required to take a pre-marriage course. My wife and I offer these classes three times a year. Each year, we intimately connect with close to 60 couples.

Some people might judge the desire of some of these couples to get married in a church, but not participate, as shallow. Others might judge *us* for being part of the wedding industry. But ask any of these couples and they'll tell you that Canadian Memorial is *their* congregation. When they get in trouble, they will turn to *their* church. Not only that, they tell their friends as they drive by, "That's my church."

Previously divorced couples sometimes come to us as a last resort. They've been given all kinds of theological reasons why they can't get married in what they had previously considered to be their church. But as far as they're concerned, they were handed a scorpion.

Weddings can be a significant hospitality ministry. Once a year, send these couples a brochure outlining the programs you offer, an invitation to come to church, and an opportunity to financially support the life of the congregation. Ask if they'd like to receive the e-newsletter.

The same holds for baptism. As Christians, we have some pretty lofty notions about what baptism means to us, but telling a couple that we won't baptize their child because they're not "members" sends a clear message about hospitality.

I've done battle with grandparents who are members of the congregation and who want their grandchildren baptized, even though the parents have no intention of bringing the children to church. I've done battle with people "cold-calling" various churches to see if they can find one that will get their children "done." All these people know is that their child is a gift from God and they're looking for ways to acknowledge that publicly. All the theology in the world just goes flying over their heads. These are battles I lost and I'm grateful for it. These people are asking for bread.

Faith Formation

Just as I was finishing the first draft of this book, the foundations of the evangelical church of the United States were rocked by the release of a book by Willow Creek Church. Willow Creek is the one of the fastest growing churches in the U.S., with over 10,000 members and counting. The book, *Reveal: Where Are You?*, was co-authored by the executive pastor, Greg Hawkins, and the lead pastor, Bill Hybels. After doing careful research at Willow Creek and 29 other congregations, they discovered that their basic assumptions about church programs were wrong. They had equated more programs with more participation, which they assumed would translate into a deeper love of God and love of people. But it wasn't happening.

What they discovered was what Dr. Diana Butler Bass discovered in her research: "Congregations that intentionally engage in Christian practices are congregations that experience new vitality." Her research pointed out that, in vital congregations, *all* the people, ministers included, are "growing members of an organic community of spiritual practice."[1] In other words, it's not mere involvement in the life of the community that forms Christian identity, it's a life of *spiritual practice*.

We've discovered a real hunger among the people of our congregation to learn the ancient practice of meditation. A married lay couple in our congregation now offers a course called Magical Mystics, an eight-week introduction to the mystical tradition and practice of prayer.

Our core curriculum always includes the practice of prayer, biblical study, theological reflection, and a leadership program focused around inner transformation. As well, we offer support groups called Be the Change, to help people articulate and enact an ecological Christian spirituality.

Authentic hospitality means offering people the Holy Spirit – opportunities to be transformed – not simply "opportunities to get involved."

Media

The media is under-utilized by the mainline church. We need to become more media savvy. If you have a program you think would interest the public, send out a news release. Make personal contact with your community papers and with the reporter who has the beat for community programming. Emerging congregations need to get their message out. If you're clergy, look for interviews for cable TV stations. Get radio spots. Make your voice known on issues. Get your mission and vision out there. Because of my last book, I'm getting a reputation as "the Green Minister." Don't let your ego get in the way of shining your light – it's not *our* light anyway, right? Let it shine.

Summary

Hospitality is only partly about being "warm and friendly." It's only partly about being "welcoming." At its core, it's about the Holy One giving the strangers in our midst, and in the world, what they are asking for – the Holy Spirit – *through us*. It's an awesome, exciting calling.

MAPPING IT OUT

Welcoming, Initiating, and Integration – the Flow

Once you've done an audit of your various entry points with beginner's mind, determine the most natural path the newcomer is likely to follow, to discover life in Christ with your congregation. Remember, they need to make a connection with six other people within the first six weeks of entering the community. Trace the natural path for each entry point. Here's an example, using the worship service as an entry point. Fred decides to try out the church that has all those signs. So Fred

- comes to church
- makes contact with the greeters
- is invited by the worship leader to join a small group
- stays for the worship service and the coffee hour
- is contacted by a small group leader or coordinator
- attends a newcomer's luncheon, where he meets staff and other newcomers (and at which personal information is gathered and entered into the congregational database)
- signs up for the e-newsletter
- receives a phone call or a personal letter from the hospitality team
- joins a small group, through which the leader discerns his next natural step – Bible study, Spirit-given gifts seminar, mission opportunity, or invitation to membership
- takes the discipleship class and the Spirit-given gifts inventory
- is commissioned to his ministry in the congregation and beyond

This process might take up to three years! (Seriously, our current board chair sat in the back pews for three years before joining the congregation.)

Now repeat this map for a person whose entry point is through the website, the mission program, the e-newsletter, or one of your faith formation programs. Are there any weak points getting in the way of this flow of initiation and integration? Of course, the process never flows as smoothly as this or in such a linear fashion. The point of the exercise is to help the hospitality team in particular, and whole congregation in general, begin to think about hospitality with beginner's mind.

---

[1] Diana Butler Bass, *Alban Weekly*, October 29, 2007.

twelve

Organizing for Emergence: A Bureaucracy of Trust

Now listen to me. I will give you counsel, and God be with you! You should represent the people before God, and you should bring their case before God; teach them the statutes and instructions and make known to them the way they are to go and the things they are to do. You should also look for able men among all the people, men who fear God, are trustworthy, and hate dishonest gain; set such men over them as officers over thousands, hundreds, fifties, and tens... If you do this, and God so commands you, you will be able to endure, and all these people shall go to their home in peace.

~ Exodus 18:19–23 ~

When a spiritual movement gets much larger than about ten people, it needs to get organized. Moses discovered this truth when he led the Hebrew people out of captivity. Jethro, his father-in-law, saw that Moses was in desperate need of a sustainable model of governance that would lead to peace in the community.

The popular cliché that contrasts "organized religion" and "spirituality" reflects a lack of clarity on the subject. When somebody says that they prefer the latter, they are communicating a couple of things. First, when they say that they reject "religion" they invariably mean the Purple through Blue values systems – tribal, warrior, and traditional. In fact, when militant atheistic scientist Richard Hawkins, cultural critic Sam Harris, and contrarian journalist Christopher Hitchens trash "religion," this is the religion they are getting apoplectic about. So, in effect, what these people are doing is communicating to the world that their own spiritual intelligence got stuck at Blue (traditional) or lower.

Second, people who like spirituality but not organized religion are often signalling that they want a commitment-free religion. They don't want to be accountable to a community of faith, and they don't want the inevitable power struggles that come with being in community, religious or secular. That's fine. But it's not mature spirituality. Getting well-organized, that is, creating the systems necessary for a culture of creative emergence, is part of authentic spirituality.

Canadian Memorial began its culture-shifting by asking the Think Tank to deliver a new organizational model within a year. It was a naïve request in the way it put the cart before the horse. But it forced the Think Tank to ask the all-important question: What are we organizing *for*? A governance model is nothing other than the crucible within which the alchemy of emergence is fostered. It's more about getting out of the way than about imposing structure.

To use a biological image, the governance "structure" should mimic the life of a cell. Dr. Bruce Lipton has broken new ground in the field of biology by recognizing that the "brains" of a cell are not contained in the nucleus, in the DNA or RNA, or in any of the other parts we were taught were the most important.[1] The brains of a cell are in its membrane. The membrane is the part that forms the boundary of the cell, through which information is allowed in and out. It interfaces with the environment, from whence all the important information originates.

In other words, the membrane acts as both the holding environment and the gatekeeper of essential information on behalf of the cell.

A governance system acts like the cell membrane. It's the "brains" or the central organizing system. It determines what information is essential for the optimal functioning of the system, and what is extraneous. It acts on behalf of the system to keep it "on purpose." It knows what to do with important information and ensures that the right people act it on. It's permeable and flexible. It allows for change, as long as the change is in the direction of a deeper and more sophisticated manifestation of itself. In other words, the governance system is responsible for the evolution of a congregation's self-definition or identity. It defines the boundaries of the organization, yet at the same time interfaces and is open to the influence of multiple environments – the congregation, the larger community, the city or town, its nation, the state of the world, and through all of these, the Holy *One*.

PRINCIPLES FOR ORGANIZING

We had three overarching principles that our governance model would need to facilitate:

1. ministry anywhere, anytime, by anybody
2. getting out of meetings and into ministry
3. spiritual gift-based service.

I first came across these principles through the wonderful work of Bill Easum and Tom Bandy. Underlying all three of these principles is the biological dynamic of self-organization. Life knows how to do life. People know how to give and receive what they need to thrive. The system will find ingenious ways to get something done. Trust it. Get out of the way as much as possible.

1. Ministry Anywhere, Anytime, by Anybody

An organizational model needs to signal that we're all "ministers" and therefore we're all responsible for taking ministry initiative. If God is calling an individual or team to do something, let's make the turn-around-time as fast as possible.

A colleague of mine shared a story from a congregation she once served. A relative newcomer had an idea for a start-up ministry. She wanted to start a soup kitchen for the poor single moms in her neighbourhood, whom she saw lining up at food banks. Naïvely, my colleague agreed. Within a few weeks, the newcomer had the local hospital donating food and a team of people ready to serve. Notices were posted around the community and the doors were opened. The moms showed up. It was all great – until the outreach committee heard about it. They met once a month for breakfast and to talk *about* mission. Well, at their next meeting they wondered who had given permission for this program, was it properly insured, and who was this newcomer anyway? They decided the program would have to be suspended until these matters could get sorted out. The next meeting was in a month. Then it would have to go to the church board for approval. The board wasn't scheduled to meet for yet a few more weeks. The woman left my colleague's congregation to attend the Baptist church. In this instance, the governance model actually discouraged ministry initiative!

At Canadian Memorial, all of our significant outreach ministries have come from individuals, not from standing committees. Our Street Meals ministry emerged when Joanne and Sallie read an article about "Mom," a woman who rides a scooter through downtown Vancouver, 365 days a year, feeding street kids stew and sandwiches, and a double portion of God's love. Thus began an eight-year (and counting) ministry to support "Mom's" work with street kids. Our Out of the Cold ministry, which involves making stew and serving people in Vancouver's poorest neighbourhood, happened when Linda's heart was moved. Our music minister organized a peace concert in memory of the 25th anniversary of John Lennon's death, in six weeks. The night of the concert, we had to turn people away. Our prayer shawl ministry was initiated by one of our members. Honestly, there are too many examples to list. But here's the important piece. These programs weren't generated from on high. It's not the job of the board to create mission programs. Or of standing committees. And it's not the job of the minister, either! This principle of ministry anywhere, anytime, by anybody is now embedded in the Christ field of our congregation.

A couple of caveats. These ministry initiatives need to fall within the parameters of our vision, mission, and values. Also, we ask that the leaders of the initiatives be members of the congregation. This ensures that they can fairly represent our culture and that they are acting in the spirit of Christ. Typically, people present their ideas to one of our paid staff. Our only question concerns the support they require. We'll help them build a team if asked. If they need start-up money, we'll try to provide that as well. We are fortunate to have a New Ministry Fund for precisely this reason. We ran a capital campaign ten years ago and committed one-third of the money we raised for this purpose.

2. Out of Meetings and into Ministry

Getting people out of meetings and into ministry is self-explanatory. We downsized from a board of 35 to a board of nine. We eliminated all committees, except for two: finance and property (including a stewardship team), and ministry and personnel. We call these our *core teams*.

We have many other teams of people who meet for specific, time-limited mission-oriented tasks. They meet as necessary. We call these *ministry teams*. Ministry teams are self-starting, self-organizing, and time-limited. If the ministry comes to an end, the team stops meeting. Meetings are held as needed. Among these ministry teams is a *worship team* and a *faith formation team*. The worship team meets primarily for the purpose of providing feedback about worship, and getting organized for the year. The faith formation team organizes our programs and publishes our Spiritual Pathways brochure once a year. Currently, we have approximately 35 of these ministry teams (not to be confused with either standing committees or small groups).

None of these teams, including the core teams, are represented on the board. It could happen that a team leader will be on the board, but such an occurrence does not happen by design, and these people do not report to the board on the work of their team. The reason for this will be explained below. In the membership model of church, being on a committee or on the board was a sign of belonging. In a discipleship model, doing ministry, not attending meetings, takes precedence.

I also meet for lunch once a month with a *management team* – composed of the chairs of our core teams: finance and property (including stewardship), ministry and personnel, and the board. This lunch meeting typically lasts an hour. The management team has no executive powers and the meeting itself is a time for fellowship and exchange of information. (See Appendix 2 for a flow chart of our organizational model.)

3. Gift-Based Ministry

"Don't ask what the world needs. Ask what makes you come alive, and go do it. Because what the world needs are people who have come alive." Howard Thurman got it right. As much as possible, we want people doing what they feel called to do, not what they think they *should* be doing. There's a difference between community service, giving back, pitching in, helping out, doing your part, volunteering – all good things – and gift-based ministry. True, these things might not *look* any different. The job is getting done one way or another and "getting the job done" is good. However, expressing your inner radiance in Christ through Spirit-infused service is better. The difference is often the presence of joy.

Paul discovered that the Body of Christ received what it needed in order to thrive through Spirit-given gifts. Gifts of teaching, healing, proclaiming, prophecy, helping, leading, shepherding, etc., were distributed throughout the community. Discerning these gifts was central to the life of the early church.

Mainline churches have largely stopped expecting the Spirit to dole out these gifts for the building up of the Body of Christ. Expect some resistance. It's a relatively new idea for many mainline congregations. We're a pragmatic bunch, after all. Many church people who have been around for a while will tell you that *somebody* needs to make the coffee and wash the cups after the service. Call it a gift if you like, but if you don't mind, I'll just roll up my sleeves and get it done. There's some truth to this, but if you pay careful attention, not everybody is on coffee duty after church. There are those men and women who never take "their turn" in the kitchen. Instead, they're talking to newcomers over a cup of coffee, or attending a post-service seminar. And it's a good thing they are – why would we want people in the kitchen who'd rather be just about anywhere else?

At Canadian Memorial, we started talking about Spirit-given gifts rather than spiritual gifts because many people associate Christianity with false modesty. "Me! Spiritually gifted? No, I'm just a humble servant." Maybe the language of spiritual gifts put too much pressure on them to make good on the gift. It was easier to imagine that the gift was *given* – they weren't born with it. Also, it shifts the focus from the gifted to the gift-giver – the Spirit. Personally, I think all of it is the ego tap-dancing. We are called to get out of the way, to die to our egos so that our most authentic self, centred in Christ, may creatively manifest.

What we want is to get people lighting up and giving back from within. When people are serving from the place of Spirit, they manifest a different quality of service characterized by joy and authenticity. So a couple of times a year our coordinator of Spirit-given gifts program leads a seminar to help people discern and deploy their gifts for ministry. We follow up with a commissioning worship service, at which we have each person kneel and receive the laying on of hands as we name their gifts, acknowledge that they are blessed by Spirit, and commission them to specific areas of service in the church and in the world; for example, "Mary-Jane, this congregation affirms that you have the gift of creativity. By the power of the Holy Spirit we commission you to claim and enact your gifts in our congregation, through the prayer shawl ministry, the drama team, and the choir."

This is the most effective way I know of breaking down the myth that the only "ministers" in the congregation are the ones who are paid.

To discern people's gifts, we use a spiritual gift inventory that is a synthesis of the work of a colleague, the Rev. David Ewart, and of an inventory developed by Bill Easum. As well, we've added our own questions and gifts that more closely reflect our culture and the areas of ministry specific to Canadian Memorial. Our evangelical brothers and sisters develop most spiritual gift inventories. Direct imports just don't work very well for our values system. For example, we've excluded some of the biblical gifts, such as speaking in tongues and miracles, and have added others, such as creativity that includes art, music, crafts, and so on.

Good governance serves these three principles of ministry anywhere, anytime, by anybody; getting people out of meetings and into ministry; and gift-based ministry. The model I present below is the most effective one I've come across in creating a structure that liberates the whole people of God to be leaders in ministry.

Being in Christ is not a spectator sport. It means finding the key that turns on the power from within. It is about catching the wave of the evolutionary Spirit. It is about growing and serving, and stepping up to *be* the presence of the emerging future. Clergy do not do this on behalf of the congregation. They enable disciples of Christ to be the "living stones" upon which the sacred temple of the emergent future is being constructed.

An effective governance model serves this end. It trusts the principle of emergence. Each of us is a radiant expression of the Holy One. An inner sacred intelligence that encompasses heart and mind yearns to manifest through our communities. This intelligence we call the Christ. By attuning ourselves to the Christ, we become centres of divine emergence.

THE POLICY GOVERNANCE MODEL OF JOHN CARVER[2]

This brings us to policy.

Policy? Policy! How can I write about all these spiritual principles and then talk about policy? Isn't this religion at its worst? Dry, spiritless, and boring?

Typically, policies are what we put in place to deal with an emergency, so if it ever comes up again we'll know "the policy." The problem is that the board changes every few years, and when the issue *does* reappear nobody can remember what the policy is or where to find it. That's policy potpourri, not policy governance.

Properly understood and executed, governing through policy is liberating. It's the most effective governance model I've come across in 20 years of ministry. In fact, it made me realize that until I discovered this model, I didn't know what I was doing. (Why isn't governance taught in seminary?) For the most part, congregations didn't know what they were doing either – not really. They thought they did, but they didn't. It made for a lot of confusion.

The basic problems with most boards centre on four areas:

1. accountability
2. focus on the past
3. lack of clarity about roles and responsibilities
4. agenda setting

1. Accountability

Until we started using policy governance, I was confused about accountability. The truth is, in my denomination, most clergy aren't really accountable. I had always noticed that my brother, a senior manager for a photocopy company, is held accountable in many ways that I, as a minister, am not. He is held accountable for staff, evaluations, a budget, and delivering on quotas. If something goes wrong, the company knows where to look. In contrast, if expenditures exceed revenues in a congregation, who is accountable: the finance committee, the stewardship committee, the board, the minister, everybody?

When everybody shares responsibility, nobody is actually accountable. Governing through clearly written policies makes accountability transparent.

When I first realized that a policy governance system would require me to be more accountable, I must admit I was stricken with fear. I knew how my brother felt. I knew how the rest of the world felt.

Why ministers shouldn't be held accountable to clearly articulated policies is a mystery to me. This lack of accountability is also very confusing to outsiders. They ask, "So who's the boss?" What they mean is, "Who do I talk to around here to get something done?" It's a fair question and one that in my experience is rarely answered clearly.

In a great many congregations, the minister is, in fact, typically *not* given authority to act on operational matters, yet she is de facto "the boss," either making decisions or influencing them in a certain direction. Outsiders thus assume she has this authority, but it's not explicitly granted, and so this crazy dance goes on. If it's a difficult decision, the minister can always defer to a committee. Often, a ridiculously simple decision gets deferred until one committee or another can get around to dealing with it. If the minister makes a decision to spend $200 on office supplies, the committee in charge of office supplies feels diminished. Policy governance makes it crystal clear that the minister, or whoever is assigned this responsibility, has authority over operational matters, within clearly proscribed limits. Although this may sound onerous, it's not. In fact, I find it a great relief to know what I'm accountable for, and what is none of my business.

2. Focus on the Past

The typical board focuses on the past. This is because most boards are composed of what John Carver calls "constituency members," meaning that board members represent a particular constituency. So, typically, the chairs of the various standing committees comprise the board, along with representatives from the women's auxiliary, the librarian, the greeter's team, etc. This in turn means that an inordinate amount of meeting time gets spent on "reporting." The representative of each committee or group naturally feels like s/he needs to report what they've been up to, to justify their existence for the past month. The other board members listen in and get the inside-scoop. (This has been the perk of being on the board – access to all the juicy information and being "in-the-know.") Two hours go by, everybody has made their report, and the energy in the room is funereal. Attendance at board meetings is chronically low, because nobody likes funerals. "Let the dead bury the dead," as Jesus said, perhaps with a wink. In policy governance, each board member represents the whole congregation, not a particular constituency.

The one positive feature about a constituency member model is communication – everybody hears what's going on in the church. But this isn't the purpose of a board meeting, and there are others ways to communicate. Often, an executive committee is appointed because the board itself is too unwieldy, or because so much attention is given to the past month's reports that no real decisions get made, or there's sensitive business that shouldn't be dealt with at the board.

But there are problems with having an executive committee, in my experience. Besides requiring yet another meeting for the core leaders, it signals to the board that all the important decisions get made elsewhere, and renders the board little more than a meeting to hear reports – which focus on the past. And we wonder why board attendance is so poor!

3. Lack of Clarity about Roles and Responsibilities

Because most boards are unclear about their role, people end up brainstorming new programs, forming sub-committees to implement these new ideas, listening to the problems that the stewardship committee is having, and then trying to rescue them by telling them about the latest visitation program. Everybody pipes in with an idea and then a decision has to be made about who will execute it. Not the minister – she's too busy already. So the chair asks for volunteers and when nobody puts up a hand, somebody asks Fred if he'll take it on. They might even start planning the agenda for the first meeting. People pull BlackBerries out of briefcases and 20 minutes later a date has been set. Most people know intuitively that they shouldn't be dealing with this at the board, but it's unclear what they *should* be dealing with, so nobody stops the madness.

4. Agenda Setting

Setting agendas for meetings is often a hellish task, because everybody assumes that their own committee's work is the most important. Therefore, if an item is left off an agenda, it signals that maybe the work of that committee is *not* as important as someone else's and feelings get hurt. I've been at board meetings where it took 20 minutes to decide whether to serve fair-trade coffee after church and whether to charge for it. It's not that the issue of fair-trade coffee is unimportant. It's incredibly important. But it doesn't belong on a board agenda.

So what does? On what basis does a board chair decide that an item is agenda-worthy? Again, it's usually very subjective, with the result that the board's agenda is too often emergency driven. The basement flooded, the roof leaked, Sunday school attendance is low, the office was broken into over the weekend, the daycare that rents space during the week is asking for lower rent. On and on it goes. Does this item belong on the agenda of a board meeting? Why? Why not? In policy governance, there are no emergencies at the board level. Setting the agenda is simplified. (See Appendix 3 for a draft copy of a typical policy governance agenda at Canadian Memorial.)

NUTS AND BOLTS

John Carver developed policy governance. His most accessible and practical book on the topic is called *Reinventing Your Board*. I recommend it highly. Here I will provide just a brief overview of the model.

Policies are written statements that address four distinct areas:

1. Ends: Ends policies describe what difference the church intends to make, for whom, and at what cost. They should reflect your vision, mission, and values statements.

2. Executive limitations: These are what the executive (typically the minister) may *not* do to achieve those ends. (More about why this is negatively stated below.)
3. Board-minister relationship: These policies detail how power is delegated by the board to the minister, staff team, or others, as well as how and when this delegated authority will be monitored.
4. Governance process: These policies describe the board's job, how it intends to conduct itself, what it expects from its members, including the chair, and how it will monitor itself.

1. Ends

Ideally your "ends policy" should be drawn from your vision, mission, and values. By *ends* Carver means the difference an organization intends to make, for whom, and at what cost. Cost relates to budget, of course. But in congregational life, it could also very well mean establishing a priority policy that will emphasize one area of the mission statement at the cost of attention to another area. At Canadian Memorial, we have a clearly stated priority policy as a sub-category of our ends policy. Our current priority policy makes explicit what is expected of the minister in relation to the growth the congregation and the types of programs we will offer (related to our mission to teach a progressive Christian faith, act for peace, and nurture loving community). The board monitors me against these priorities annually, and only on the basis of how well I have achieved these priorities.

This is an enormous relief for me. Previously, I set my own *goals* – goals are *means*, by the way, not *ends* – and then a team of people representing a cross-section of the congregation assessed whether I had achieved them. This was difficult for them because they could only comment on where their lives had intersected with mine.

But even this is more monitoring of the minister than takes place in many congregations. Prior to our adoption of policy governance, the board played virtually no role in establishing priorities or in monitoring our vision and mission. Today, I am crystal clear about what the congregation wants me to focus my limited energies on achieving, and in turn I can set up the teams I need in order to meet these ends.

One of the frequent criticisms of the Carver model is that it gives the minister too much power. This is not my experience. Remember, the board, on behalf of the congregation, delegates all authority. A minister would be crazy not to delegate tasks to various ministry teams in order to meet the ends policies.

For example, I am accountable for a balanced budget, so I make sure I have chartered accountants and MBAs who know their way around finances. (I *don't* know my way around finances, but I can tell you that in the last few years, since I've been made accountable, I've learned a lot about reading a financial sheet.) I am also responsible for presenting the budget, but I always ask for a member of my finance team to do it. Still, it's my responsibility at the end of the day.

In other words, just because it's my responsibility to make sure something gets done doesn't mean that I have to do all the work myself. On the ground, I set up exactly the teams needed to achieve the priorities given to me by the board on behalf of the congregation. Trust is required in both directions. Not only does the congregation need to trust its minister and refuse the temptation to micromanage, but the minister must also trust the expertise and capacity of the people of the congregation to accomplish the priorities of the congregation.

Determining ends policies is hard work. And it's easy to confuse *means* with *ends*. *Ends* are the results. *Means* are how you achieve those results. Programs and services are almost always means, not ends.

Ends also are not the same as good intentions. Carver recommends removing all verbs such as *support, assist, and advocate*. They don't describe the difference you intend to make in the lives of people. Carver has a great rule of thumb: "If your statement describes your organization's actions rather than the benefit to be received by the consumer, they signify means. Teaching children to read is means; children *can* read is ends."[3]

In the course of writing this book, I realized that our mission statement that says, "We teach a progressive Christian faith," is actually a means statement. *Teaching* is a means. If we change this statement to read, "Disciples of Christ will articulate and enact an openhearted and open-minded Christian faith," we're closer to what Carver means by "ends" statement, because it describes the benefit to the recipient and the difference we're making in the world.

Take the second element required of an ends statement: *for whom*? This makes for an important conversation. For whom do we exist? Our own congregation? The unchurched in the surrounding neighbourhood? Families with children? Spiritual seekers? Youth? Thirty- to 45-year-olds? Does our website ministry extend our reach to an international constituency? All of the above?

If it's the latter, can we actually achieve this end with limited resources? What are we willing to give up in order to achieve this result? This is the cost criterion of an ends statement.

Don't rush this process. It may take a year to develop an ends policy that truly reflects your intentions. Carver encourages organizations to start by developing the other three policy areas first, while developing the ends policies.

2. Executive Limitations

The board is responsible to develop and oversee all these policy areas, but it turns over the *means* of achieving these ends to staff – in our case, the minister. In other words, the means could also be a management team of laypeople. For the purposes of this chapter, I will assume that it is the minister who carries out these executive functions. She has the executive function of employing any means necessary to achieve the ends policy, within certain parameters. These parameters are clearly laid out in the executive limitations policy – a statement of what the minister may *not* do to achieve the ends: for example, break the law, violate the Human Rights Code, exceed the budget by $5000, be nasty to the secretary... You get the idea. As long as a policy is *reasonably interpreted,* the minister is free to make it happen in any way she sees fit, without interference or the need for permission from the board. This is why I called this chapter "A Bureaucracy of Trust."

As noted above, these executive limitations are stated proscriptively rather than prescriptively. They don't tell the minister *how* to achieve the ends. In fact, policy governance specifically forbids micromanagement. Rather, they clarify what may *not* be done in order to achieve them. We find the same principle in the Ten Commandments. There's incredible freedom implicit in telling a person what they may *not* do. Don't kill, steal, treat your parents badly, or cheat on your wife. Other than those restrictions, go and sin boldly. Stating what may *not* be done helps the board resist the temptation to micromanage. The minister, not the board, is responsible for *means.*

3. Board–Minister Relationship

At the highest level, this policy ensures that the board connects to the operations of the congregation *through the minister.* I can't tell you how many times the chair of our board finds herself redirecting questions and issues to me: "You'll have to ask Bruce about that; he's the minister." The chair has her own responsibilities, but management of the operations is not one of them.

"But isn't the minister supposed to deal with 'spiritual matters' and leave the rest to us?" people will ask. The health and optimal functioning of the Body of Christ *is* a spiritual matter. The budget *is* a profoundly spiritual matter. The state of the facilities conveys a lot to the public about the spirituality of the congregation. In other words, the "spiritual matters" versus "operational matters" distinction is false.

"But doesn't this give the minister too much power?" Remember, the board holds all the power and is ultimately accountable to the congregation. The only power the minister has is delegated power. If the board is anxious about how the minister exercises power in any area, they are free to write more restrictive executive limitations policies.

Within this high-level policy, other clarifying policies are then embedded: for example, only decisions of the board as a whole, and not individual board members, are binding on the minister; the board will be clear with the minister about ends and about what may not be done in achieving them (executive limitations); the minister will be rigorously monitored against the ends policies and the ends policies alone; the frequency and method of monitoring will be established as policy; as long as the minister reasonably interprets policy, s/he is authorized to "establish all further policies, make all decisions, take all actions, establish all practices and develop all activities."[4]

Each month I am required to sign off on one or more of the policies for which I am responsible. As part of this sign-off process, I present evidence to show that I am in compliance. In this way, an annual cycle of policy review is established, and this itself is included in the policy manual.

4. Governance Process

This policy area articulates what the board is supposed to do, and not do, on behalf of the congregation. Within that high-level statement, other policies will be embedded that clarify the style of governing.

For example, these policies will clearly articulate the three areas already discussed (ends, executive limitations, and board-minister relations), as well as the governance process itself.

They may also specify how members will be trained in policy governance, emphasize vision over internal preoccupation, encourage diversity of viewpoints, be future-oriented rather than past-oriented, require that the board speak with one voice to the congregation, define the board chair's role as assuring the integrity of the board's process, and stress the importance of listening to the congregation.

BOARD RECRUITMENT

When we made the shift to policy governance, our board membership went from 35 members to nine. This was possible because we were no longer operating from a constituency-based model, where every committee needs to be represented on the board. Recruiting board members was no longer a last-minute, desperate scramble to find enough people to serve.

In fact, we now have time to interview each potential candidate. Being on the board takes on much more significance for people because we interview each person against specific criteria:

• board attendance (missing more than two meetings in a row could mean dismissal)
• regular attendance at worship
• a spiritual practice
• exemplary behaviour in the community, and
• tithing (giving regularly and proportionately of their income)

We discuss each criterion at the interview. This signals that they are committing to a culture of high expectation. Far from scaring people away, natural leaders will respond positively and enthusiastically.

LISTENING TO THE CONGREGATION

The board monitors itself against the criterion of "listening to the congregation," and the success of this model depends upon how well it executes this function. As mentioned, one of the pluses of the constituency-based model is that more people get to hear about everything that is taking place in the congregation through the committee reports. When this reporting is eliminated, there will be a communication vacuum that needs to be addressed.

Addressing this vacuum requires the use of both formal and informal tools. Informally, board members are involved in every aspect of congregational life and are therefore able to keep an ear to the ground about the mood and morale of the congregation. They listen in on conversations before worship and at the coffee hour, they engage in parking lot conversations after meetings and Bible study, and so on. More formally, we hold regularly scheduled "Fireside Chats" after the church service, to give people an opportunity to ask questions of the board. In a previous chapter, I wrote about the importance of newsletters, whether electronic or printed. Suggestion boxes may be placed in the sanctuary or in the church offices.

In other words, we make it clear that we welcome feedback and that we will respond to it. Questionnaires that elicit feedback about specific policies are useful. A World Café process is a great way to listen to the congregation. If the congregation does not feel that it is being heard, distrust may grow. Therefore, we are always on the lookout for creative ways to listen to the community.

Let me be clear. At the end of this process you will end up with a policy manual. Ours is a 38-page document. All the board members will have their own copy, and one will be left in the office for anyone who is interested. (We also post ours on our website.) Everyone will be able to find anything they could ever want to know about why you exist and how you operate in this manual.

Having said that, it may come as good news to you that you don't need to re-create the wheel with this policy manual. We used another church's manual as the template for our own. The main difference will be in the ends section of the manual. You can find our manual at www.canadianmemorial.org. Feel free to use it as a template. You can find another carefully prepared manual at www.gilmorepark.org.

---

[1] Bruce Lipton, *The Biology of Belief*, (Santa Rosa: Mountain of Love/Elite Books, 2005), 75ff.
[2] John Carver, *Reinventing Your Board: A Step-by-Step Guide to Implementing Policy Governance* (San Francisco: Jossey-Bass, 1997).
[3] Ibid., 131.
[4] Ibid., 123.

Conclusion

BLESSED UNREST

*There is vitality, a life force, an energy, a quickening that
is translated through you into action, and because there is
only one of you in all time, this expression is unique...
You have to keep open and aware directly to the urges that
motivate you. Keep the channel open. There is no satisfaction
whatever at any time. There is only a queer, divine
dissatisfaction, a blessed unrest that keeps us marching and
makes us more alive...*[1]

~ MARTHA GRAHAM TO AGNES DE MILLE, *DANCE TO THE PIPER* ~

*Foxes have holes, and birds of the air have nests,
but the Son of Man has nowhere to lay his head.*

~ LUKE 9:58 ~

Congregations are centres of creative emergence. Our consent to be
vessels of Christ's spirit means that the "new thing" God is doing in
the world has an opportunity to come into being through us. This
new thing is evolutionary in nature, following the same fundamental
principles and dynamics as this 14-billion-year-old, Spirit-infused
universe.

In the opening quote, Martha Graham describes the evolutionary impulse present in all of us and in every congregation. This "divine dissatisfaction" is infused with Spirit. This is what makes the unrest "blessed." In every realm, from the geological to the biological; to the social, cultural, and spiritual domains of human experience; Spirit irrepressibly seeks out new forms and fuller expressions of itself. An emergent culture taps into the blessed unrest that is the evolutionary Spirit of the Christ – transcending and including previous innovations; self-organizing; and embracing novelty, the emergence of new forms.

In this book, I have suggested that it is possible to intentionally foster a culture wherein the living Spirit of Christ may light us up from within. When this happens, ministry opportunities begin to multiply. The congregation I serve is small compared to many in North America. And yet I am always amazed by the number of people who are willing to both generate and then execute new initiatives in the name of Christ and the service of humanity.

Jesus taught that he had no place to rest his head and that once a person set her hand to the plough there was no looking back – at least not for those "fit for the kingdom" (Luke 9:62). Before I began to think through an evolutionary lens, I always felt sorry for Jesus, lacking a bed or a home where he could rest his head. But I now understand this teaching metaphorically. Jesus was caught up in an evolutionary momentum, which drove him to become an ever-fuller manifestation of the Holy *One*, and to help others be the same. To tap into this blessed unrest, as Christians, is to follow the one who had no place to rest his head. We will always be trying and failing, dying and rising, honouring tradition and then transcending it, reaching plateaus and then, by the power of the ever-renewing Spirit, looking for the next ascent.

Jesus' life, death, and resurrection informed a movement of spiritual pilgrims that continues to this day through gatherings we call congregations. But our calling is not to "be like Jesus," mimicking what he did 2000 years ago. We're not here to copy. We're here to co-create. We need to recapture the sense of being a *movement*, not a static church that exists to perpetuate structures and beliefs that may have served us well in the past.

We model Jesus' way of being when we surrender to this blessed unrest, and when we exhibit courage in pre-sensing and then presencing the unique future that needs us in order to be realized. As we do these things, we incarnate the heart and mind of the Christ, as did Jesus of Nazareth. We become the Body of Christ, his very presence in our own neighbourhoods. This can be more than a good idea. It can be a governing principle that enables our congregations to be powerful witnesses for Christ.

There are no quick fixes, no magic wands we can wave to bring about congregational transformation, and I pray that I haven't conveyed such an idea in this book. At best, this book may serve as a primer to get the juices flowing in your congregation. We've been at it 12 years at Canadian Memorial and, as the song goes, "we've only just begun." When people begin to feel this blessed unrest as the very presence of the Holy One inviting us, nudging us, cajoling us, to be the radiant presence of Christ – from the inside out – then the church comes alive. It's that simple and that challenging.

May the Holy *One*, flowing through you and your congregation, continue to bless you and to baptize you to claim and create your Christ-shaped future.

---

[1] Paul Hawkens, *Blessed Unrest* (New York: Penguin Group, U.S.A., 2007). I am grateful to Paul Hawkens for this quotation and for his new book, which uses this phrase, Blessed Unrest, as its title.

Postscript

FAILURES AND FOIBLES: THE FREEDOM TO FAIL

A scoffer who is rebuked will only hate you; the wise, when rebuked, will love you.

~ PROVERBS 9:8, SOPHIA/WISDOM ~

I distrust books that make congregational transformation out to be a cakewalk – one big happy family pulling together for the good of all. It wasn't that way in the early church and, so far, my ministry tells a different story. In truth, like any family, congregations and their leaders make lot of mistakes and missteps are the norm. In the process of leading the cultural shift at Canadian Memorial, I made more than a few mistakes myself. I want to end by naming them (some for the second time), along with some hard won lessons I learned.

1. I worked way too hard. My mistake was being naïve about how challenging this shift was going to be. In my passion to "make" this happen, I forgot a central principle of emergence: trust that the process will organically unfold. The farmer in Jesus' parable plants the seeds and *then goes to sleep!* (Mark 4:26–9). The seeds do their thing in their own sweet time. You can't rush it. In retrospect I was impatient. I came to my wife, after the first year of working 60-

hour weeks, and said, "Don't worry. It won't be like this for much longer." Three years later it finally settled down.

It's one thing to model commitment as a leader. It's another to over-function. The latter shows a lack of trust in both the lay leaders and in the dynamic of emergence. When one person is over-functioning, others are being disempowered. To give but one example, I thought that it was crucial to develop a "contemporary service" – worship band, PowerPoint, the whole nine yards. I ended up putting the first PowerPoint services together myself, playing in the band, preaching, and tap dancing while doing prayers! The service was creative, Spirit-led, transformative, and ultimately exhausting. Truly, it was a model service and all who participated said as much. It was where church needs to go in the 21st century. But it was unsustainable for all involved. We had a great team of people putting it together. But we needed four teams.

Lesson learned: Start nothing until you have the infrastructure to support it solidly in place. This is probably obvious to most people, but it wasn't to me. I wouldn't do this again unless there was a paid, accountable person – other than myself – responsible.

2. We ran a major capital campaign at the same time as we began the process of congregational renewal. Big mistake. Not because it failed. In fact, the campaign was a towering success. But it took a toll on me (and my wife).

Lesson learned: Don't do this. The process of culture shifting is sufficient unto itself. It will need all your available energy – and then some.

3. I hadn't counted on the fact that our small group and ministry team leaders would get tired, or want a new challenge after five or six years. Cultivating new leaders, whether for small groups, core teams, or ministry teams, is so important that it cannot be tagged onto the list of the minister's responsibilities. It doesn't

get done – at least not well in my case. We pay an honorarium to a coordinator of lay ministry – what the secular world calls a "volunteer coordinator." Her job is to work with staff to monitor the health of all the teams, anticipate leadership changes, recruit new leaders, and celebrate their leadership.

Lesson learned: Make succession planning a priority, put somebody in charge of it, and start a leadership training program as soon as possible. For the energy every new program requires to get going, you'll need twice as much to maintain it.

4. When we started using Carver's policy governance, the model I used was based on the Doctor of Ministry thesis of a colleague, who tried to adapt it. Basically, he reduced the size of the board, cut down on the number of meetings, and talked *about* some of the underlying principles. After eight years of trying this hybrid model, I learned for myself what Carver warns about: it doesn't work to do policy governance in half measures. We were trying to do policy governance without written policies, hoping that we could cut corners. Big mistake.

Lesson learned: If you're making the transition to policy governance, search out expert advice and guidance.

5. Finally, it took me far too long to appreciate how much intentional energy is required to "hold" newcomers. The bottom line is that churches face all manner of competition for their allegiance. At Canadian Memorial, we're in direct competition with the ocean, the mountains, Sunday morning soccer practice, Sabbath at Starbucks, and a host of other formidable adversaries. And I thought scintillating preaching was all it took!

Lesson learned: If at all possible, give this ministry dedicated staff time or create a lay ministry team to oversee it. We created the position of coordinator of hospitality to make sure there is a point person overseeing all areas of congregational life related to hospitality. Newcomers need to feel that they are connected in a network of love, if they are going to stick around. They need to know that they are missed when they don't show up, and that they are worth fighting for.

Appendix 1

CANADIAN MEMORIAL VALUES STATEMENT

We are committed to:

Peace: We promote peace, in ourselves, our relationships, and our world.

Justice: We promote justice for the disenfranchised.

Diversity: We honour personal, cultural, and religious diversity as God's intention.

Innovation: We are open to creative change as the Spirit prompts us.

Equality: We have equal, but different, gifts, as members of Christ's body.

Reverence: We treat the earth and all creation as sacred gifts of God.

Stewardship: We give back to God a portion of our time, talent, and money.

Integrity: We act on our commitments and beliefs.

Joy: We cultivate joy in our relationship with God and each other.

Appendix 2

CANADIAN MEMORIAL ORGANIZATIONAL CHART

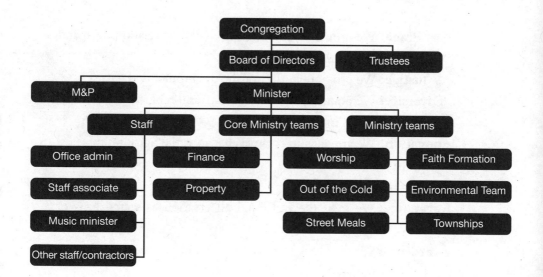

Appendix 3

SAMPLE BOARD AGENDA

Location:
Date/Time:
Snacks by:
Recorder:

Time in minutes	Description	Led by
20	**1. Gather as a Board** a) Call to order, welcome, introductions b) Opening prayer c) Approve agenda d) Approve minutes of Board meeting e) Review minutes of Congregational meeting f) Sign-up for reflections, snacks, and recording	Chair Volunteer Chair All Chair
15	**2. Spiritual Reflection** • On an aspect of our Ministry goals	Chair
30	**3. Minister Reports** a) Written report on key current issues b) General minister's limitations c) Financial condition – audit d) Legacy / Manse Funds	Minister
15	**4. Board Policy Governance** a) Review of function of the Board under this model and the basic structure of meetings b) Review policy review schedule c) Any business concerning how we operate as a Board? d) Looking ahead to the next month's policy concerns	Chair
30	**5. Listening to Our Congregation** • Focusing on our Ministry goals	All
5	**6. Board Retreat** • Saturday, Sept 8	Chair
1	**7. Adjournment**	Chair

Bibliography

Bass, Diana Butler. *Christianity for the Rest of Us: How the Neighborhood Church Is Transforming the Faith*. San Francisco: HarperSanFrancisco, 2006.

Bennis, Warren. *On Becoming a Leader*. New York: Basic Books, 2003.

Benyus, Janine M. *Biomimicry: Innovation Inspired by Nature*. New York: HarperCollins Publishers, 1997.

Borg, Marcus J. *The Heart of Christianity: Rediscovering a Life of Faith*. San Francisco: HarperSanFrancisco, 2003.

—. *Jesus, a New Vision: Spirit, Culture, and the Life of Discipleship*. 1st ed. San Francisco: Harper & Row, 1987.

—. *Meeting Jesus Again for the First Time: The Historical Jesus & the Heart of Contemporary Faith*. San Francisco: HarperSanFrancisco, 1994.

Briggs, John, and F. David Peat. *Seven Life Lessons of Chaos: Spiritual Wisdom from the Science of Change*. New York: HarperCollins Publishers, 1999.

Brown, Juanita. *The World Café: Shaping Our Futures through Conversations that Matter*. 1st ed. San Francisco: Berrett-Koehler Publishers, 2005.

Capra, Fritjof. *The Hidden Connections: A Science for Sustainable Living*. New York: Anchor Books, 2002.

Carver, John. *Boards that Make a Difference: A New Design for Leadership in Nonprofit and Public Organizations*. 2nd ed. San Francisco: Jossey-Bass, 1997.

Carver, John, and Miriam Mayhew Carver. *Reinventing Your Board: A Step-by-Step Guide to Implementing Policy Governance.* San Francisco: Jossey-Bass, 1997.

Christie, Anna S. *Evoking Change: Make a Difference in Your Life and in the World.* Lincoln: iUniverse, 2007.

Crossan, John Dominic. *The Historical Jesus: The Life of a Mediterranean Jewish Peasant.* New York: HarperCollins Publishers, 1991.

—. *Jesus: A Revolutionary Biography.* San Francisco: HarperSanFrancisco, 1994.

Easum, William M. *The Church Growth Handbook.* Nashville: Abingdon Press, 1990.

—. *Dancing with Dinosaurs: Ministry in a Hostile & Hurting World.* Nashville: Abingdon Press, 1993.

—. Herb Miller, ed. *How to Reach Baby Boomers.* Nashville: Abingdon Press, 1991.

—. *Sacred Cows Make Gourmet Burgers: Ministry Anytime, Anywhere, by Anybody.* Nashville: Abingdon Press, 1995.

Easum, William M., and Thomas G. Bandy. *Growing Spiritual Redwoods.* Nashville: Abingdon Press, 1997.

Edwards, Denis. *The God of Evolution.* New York: Paulist Press, 1999.

—. *Jesus and the Cosmos.* Eugene: Wipf & Stock Publishers, 2004.

Foss, Michael W. *Power Surge: Six Marks of Discipleship for a Changing Church.* Minneapolis: Fortress Press, 2000.

Fowler, James. W. *Weaving the New Creation: Stages of Faith and the Public Church.* Eugene: Wifp and Stock Publishers, 2001.

Fox, Matthew. *The Coming of the Cosmic Christ.* San Francisco: Harper & Row Publishers, 1988.

—. *Creativity: Where the Divine and the Human Meet.* New York: Jeremy P. Tarcher/Penguin, 2002.

—. *On Becoming a Musical, Mystical Bear: Spirituality American Style.* New York: Paulist Press/Deus Books, 1976.

Fox, Matthew, and Rupert Sheldrake. *Natural Grace: Dialogues on Creation, Darkness, and the Soul in Spirituality and Science*. New York: Doubleday, 1996.

—. *The Physics Exploring the Realm of Angels: Where Science and Spirit Meet*. San Francisco: HarperSanFrancisco, 1996.

Gribbin, John, and Martin Rees. *Cosmic Coincidences: Dark Matter, Mankind, and Anthropic Cosmology*. New York: Bantam Books, 1989.

Haught, John F. *God after Darwin: A Theology of Evolution*. Boulder: Westview Press, 2000.

Hesselbein, Frances, and Rob Johnston, eds. *On Leading Change: A Leader to Leader Guide*. San Francisco: Jossey Bass, 2002.

Johnson, Elizabeth A. *She Who Is: The Mystery of God in Feminist Theological Discourse*. New York: The Crossroad Publishing Company, 1992.

Laszlo, Ervin. *Science and the Reenchantment of the Cosmos: The Rise of the Integral Vision of Reality*. Rochester, VT: Inner Traditions, 2006.

Liebes, Sidney, et al. *A Walk through Time: From Stardust to Us*. New York: John Wiley & Sons, 1998.

Lipton, Bruce. *The Biology of Belief: Unleashing the Power of Consciousness, Matter, and Miracles*. Santa Rosa: Mountain of Love/Elite Books, 2005.

Macy, Joanna, and Molly Young Brown. *Coming Back to Life: Practices to Reconnect Our Lives, Our World*. Gabriola Island: New Society Publishers, 1998.

McKibben, Bill. *Deep Economy: The Wealth of Communities and the Durable Future*. New York: Times Books, 2007.

O'Murchu, Diarmuid. *Evolutionary Faith: Rediscovering God in Our Great Story*. Maryknoll: Orbis Books, 2004.

Robinson, Anthony B. *Transforming Congregational Culture*. Grand Rapids: William B. Eerdmans Publishing Company, 2003.

Sanguin, Bruce. *Darwin, Divinity, and the Dance of the Cosmos: An Ecological Christianity*. Kelowna: CopperHouse, 2007.

Scharmer, C. Otto. *Theory U: Leading from the Future as it Emerges*. Cambridge, MA: Sol., 2007.

Schwartzentruber, Michael, ed. *The Emerging Christian Way: Thoughts, Stories, and Wisdom for a Faith of Transformation*. Kelowna: CopperHouse, 2006.

Senge, Peter, et al. *Presence: An Exploration of Profound Change in People, Organizations, and Society*. New York: Doubleday, 2005.

Swimme, Brian. *The Hidden Heart of the Cosmos: Humanity and the New Story*. Maryknoll: Orbis Books, 1996.

—. *The Universe Is a Dragon*. Santa Fe: Bear & Company, 1984.

Swimme, Brian, and Thomas Berry. *The Universe Story From the Primordial Flaring Forth to the Ecozoic Era – A Celebration of the Unfolding of the Cosmos*. San Francisco: HarperSanFrancisco, 1992.

Wheatley, Margaret J. *Leadership and the New Science: Discovering Order in a Chaotic World*. 2nd ed. San Francisco: Berrett-Koehler Publishers, 1999.

Wilber, Ken. *The Essential Ken Wilber: An Introductory Reader*. Boston: Shambala, 1998.

—. *Sex, Ecology, Spirituality: The Spirit of Evolution*. Boston: Shambhala, 1995.

Praise for

Darwin, Divinity, and the Dance of the Cosmos: An Ecological Christianity

by Bruce Sanguin

In *Darwin, Divinity, and the Dance of the Cosmos*, Sanguin has provided a new and exciting paradigm for thinking Christians and spiritual seekers alike. He has provided a basis for a deep theological shift, a fresh cosmology, and a new way of perceiving our reality based on excellent scholarship, both scientific and biblical. And he has done that in a very readable way that is open to anyone who yearns to learn. It is on top of our recommended reading list.

~ FRED C. PLUMER, PRESIDENT, THE CENTER FOR PROGRESSIVE CHRISTIANITY

Bruce Sanguin explores, in readable style, the latest scientific insights into the origins of the universe, evoking awe and wonder at our enchanted cosmos story. While quoting from Thomas Berry and Brian Swimme, Sanguin offers an inspiring approach between science and the biblical stories of the Christian tradition. He takes us beyond our "human-centred" focus and creates an expanding and evolving ecological Christian theology... A fascinating read!

~ JUDY SCHACHTEL, GLENAIRLY - CENTRE FOR EARTH AND SPIRIT

Praise for

Summoning the Whirlwind: Unconventional Sermons for a Relevant Christian Faith

by Bruce Sanguin

While many mainline Canadian clergy play it safe and bland, Sanguin feels called to tell it like it is. He sets out what it means to stand up as a progressive Christian in the 21st century. These highly readable, even entertaining, sermons reveal the mind of an intellectual with a passion for justice. But they're also the vulnerable self-reflections of a man with a poetic sensibility and a generous spirit, including towards those with whom he strongly disagrees.

~ DOUGLAS TODD, THE VANCOUVER SUN

Also from Bruce Sanguin

Darwin, Divinity, and the Dance of the Cosmos
An Ecological Christianity
Represents a challenge to our theological and liturgical models, an exciting theological journey of discovery, and an opportunity to become *reacquainted* with the Spirit of God moving in and through the very dynamics of an unfolding universe.

Summoning the Whirlwind
Unconventional Sermons for a Relevant Christian Faith
Well-crafted, thoughtful sermons from a progressive Christian minister.

More CopperHouse books from Wood Lake Publishing

The Art of Parables
Reinterpreting the Teaching Stories of Jesus in Word & Form
CHARLES MCCOLLOUGH
Reach for this fully illustrated resource, view the photographs of the sculpture and reflect on favorite stories in a new way.
(Includes images for projection on CD)

Living the Heart of Christianity
A Guidebook for Putting Your Faith into Action
MARCUS BORG AND TIM SCORER
A companion to Borg's bestseller.

Cause for Hope
Humanity at the Crossroads
BILL PHIPPS with a foreword by David C. Korten, author of *The Great Turning*
This provocative book by one of the most provocative leaders in the church challenges the governing story that has shaped and defined Western culture and society.

The Emerging Christian Way
Thoughts, Stories, and Wisdom for a Faith of Transformation
MICHAEL SCHWARTZENTRUBER, ED.
A bestseller with contributions from some of the leading authors and creative thinkers in the field of developing Christianity such as, Marcus Borg, Tom Harpur, Sallie McFague, Matthew Fox and Thomas Berry, Bill Phipps, Bruce Harding, Tim Scorer, Nancy Reeves, and Bruce Sanguin.

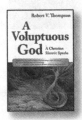

A Voluptuous God
A Christian Heretic Speaks
ROBERT V. THOMPSON
Gives access to the larger spiritual truths that our minds and souls dance with daily and that give shape and meaning to our lives.

Oil & Water
Two Faiths : One God
AMIR HUSSAIN
Written by a Muslim for Christians, this book looks at the truths of two great faith traditions.

Christianity
A New Look at Ancient Wisdom
DAVID J. H. HART
A comprehensive look at a revitalized Christian faith.

Dispatches from the Global Village
DEREK EVANS
Informing, challenging, and inspiring columns from world traveller and former Deputy Secretary General of Amnesty International, Derek Evans.

Available at fine bookstores or call Wood Lake Publishing at 1.800.663.2775 or visit www.woodlakebooks.com

Experience! FAITH FORMATION CURRICULUM FOR ADULTS

Experiencing
THE BIBLE AGAIN FOR THE FIRST TIME

Also available:

Experiencing Jesus
Based on Marcus Borg's *Jesus: Uncovering the Life, Teachings, and Relevance of a Religious Revolutionary.*

Coming next in the series

Experiencing
AN ECOLOGICAL CHRISTIANITY
Based on Bruce Sanguin's
Darwin, Divinity, and the Dance of the Cosmos:
An Ecological Christianity
Available August 2008

Order from Wood Lake Publishing – www.woodlakebooks.com

TOLL-FREE PHONE 1.800.663.2775 | **TOLL-FREE FAX 1.888.841.9991** | info@woodlakebooks.com